Hobbies for Men

Manly Men Doing Manly Things
Revised 2016

By: D.L. Haley

D.L. Haley

Hobbies for Men: Manly Men Doing Manly Things; Revised 2016, copyright © 2016 Mix Books, LLC
mix-booksonline.com

Published by Mix Books, LLC

This is a work of fiction. Names, characters, places and incidents are the product of the author's imagination or are used fictitiously, and any resemblance to actual persons, living or dead, business, companies, events, or locales is entirely coincidental.

Hobbies for Men

Dedicated to the men who embrace the confidence, skills, and virtues of manliness.

Table of Contents

ENRICHMENT 9
- ASTRONOMY 9
- ANTIQUES 10
- CALLIGRAPHY 12
- CONJURING / MAGIC 13
- LANGUAGES 15
- ROCKS AND FOSSILS 15
- RUBIX 16
- TRAVELING 17
- WRITING 18

PHYSICAL 21
- BLACKSMITHING 21
- BOXING 22
- FENCING 23
- HORSES 24
- MARTIAL ARTS & MIXED MARTIAL ARTS 25
- ROWING 27
- SKYDIVING 28
- SPORTS COACH 29
- WINGSUIT FLYING 30
- WRESTLING 31

SOCIAL 33
- AMATEUR THEATRICS 33
- BALLROOM DANCING 34
- BIG BROTHER 35
- BOARD GAMES 35
- CAMPANOLOGY 36
- CIVIL WAR REENACTOR 37
- DARTS 38
- HAM RADIO 39

    Larping 40
    Podcaster 41
    Pool 42
    Public speaking 43
    Poker 43

CREATIVE 45

    Carpentry 45
    Cooking 46
    Drumming 47
    Duct tape art 48
    Glass blowing 49
    Handmade crafts and art 49
    Home brewing 50
    Leatherworking (also called Leather Crafting) 52
    Model ship building 53
    Musical instruments 54
    Photography and Lomography 55
    Sculpting from junk 57
    Silversmithing 58
    Whittling 59

OUTDOORS 61

    Archery 61
    Backpacking 61
    Beekeeping 62
    Camping 63
    Cowboy 64
    Cycling and mountain biking 65
    Falconry 67
    Fishing 68
    Flying 69
    Gardening 70
    Gold panning 72
    Hot air ballooning 73

- Kayaking 75
- Marathon running 76
- Motorcycling/BMX biking 78
- Paddle Boarding 79
- Rock climbing 81
- Sailing 83
- Scuba diving 84
- Snowboarding 85
- Spelunking 86
- Storm chasing 87
- Surfing 88
- Survivalism 89
- Target Shooting 90
- White water rafting 91

UNUSUAL 93
- Bad movies 93
- Bricklaying 94
- Extreme ironing 95
- Geocashing 96
- Ghost hunting 96
- Lock picking 98
- Jousting 99
- News-raiding 100
- Robot making 101
- Taphophilia 102
- Tomahawk and Axe throwing 102
- Volcano boarding 104
- Whip cracking 105

EVERYTHING ELSE 107
- Black powder cannons 107
- Car racing 109
- Chess 110
- Cigars 111

D.L. Haley

COLLECTIBLES	112
COMBINE DEMOLITION DERBY	113
DRONES	114
HOME IMPROVEMENT	115
MODEL RAILROADING	116
PINBALL	117
RESTORE A CLASSIC CAR	118
PLANE SPOTTING	120
RIDING ROLLER COASTERS	120
SLOT CAR RACING	121
STAND-UP COMEDY	122
VENTRILOQUISM	123
AUTHOR'S NOTES	**125**

Enrichment
(Improve the Mind)

Astronomy

One of my ambitions is to have a small observatory. It's a long way off but I'd like a dome of some sort, just because it seems more futuristic. There is a ton of information online for observatory kits in dome and sky shed form (sky sheds have roll-back roofs). Just search for 'observatory for amateur' and see what comes up.

Anyway, back to the actual astronomy, or stargazing as many hobbyists call it. Astronomy is simply watching the sky for celestial objects such as planets, nebulae, meteor showers and star clusters, as well as sunspots and eclipses. You will need a telescope but a good beginner's scope can be found for under $200. I recently saw the highly rated Celestron PowerSeeker 114EQ Newtonian Reflector Telescope for $133. As you get into your hobby more you'll want to upgrade to something more powerful with all the bells and whistles but always look around. There's a huge range of prices on the net for the same instrument.

Before you spend a dime, though, start at the library. Read all you can, look through star charts and just use your binoculars to look up to get a sense of whether this is your thing. Astronomy is primarily an outdoor hobby, though also an intellectual one. And if you're not a night owl perhaps you should rethink this as a pastime. Keep in mind, however, that's it really quite cool to be able to look up to the night sky and casually say, "Oh, there's Ursa Major."

Not surprisingly the internet offers up masses of information on astronomy. I suggest you start with Amateur Astronomy Magazine, at this address:

http://www.amateurastronomy.com/.

Antiques

The first rule of antique buying for your own collection is "Buy what you like." You may think that ugly old lamp will appreciate in value, but do you really want to be looking at it on your shelf for the next 20 years? And before buying anything, do some due diligence or you could end up with a real lemon.

Over the years I've had a few good buys when I've gone on instinct alone. Like the original Grace Line cruise poster I bought for three dollars in a thrift store because I thought it would look good in my den. A few years later I sold it for well over $400. Turned out it was designed by Jo Mora and was highly collectible. Today, that same poster could fetch $800. The thing is, I was just plain lucky. I had no idea of the value of the poster when I bought it, and I can tell you I've bought far more lemons than golden eggs over the years.

Technically, that poster was "vintage," not "antique." In the trade an antique is considered to be at least 100 years old, but many people either unwittingly or deliberately label their vintage products as antique.

Many antique collectors focus on a specific type of object or period. Furniture or furnishings like glassware, silver, or carpets; ceramics/porcelain; pottery; clocks; jewelry; metalware/metal works; etc., are some of the types of antiques that collectors buy. Antiques from another country, such as Asian antiques, are popular and tend to rise in value.

Antiques can be found at yard sales, flea markets, estate sales, and auctions, where you should not be paying the high end antique dealer's markup.

Here's a useful resource for buying and selling antiques:

D.L. Haley

http://antiques.about.com/od/buyingandsellingantiques/u/BuyingSelling.htm.

To learn more, look for a local antique or collectors club near you on www.Yelp.com or on www.meetup.com and check your local library for antique buyers' guides.

Calligraphy

Calligraphy is an ancient visual and writing art using calligraphy pens and specialized nibs. During the Middle Ages, men carefully used calligraphy to transcribe existing books of the day. In Asia, men used calligraphy to classically and skillfully express themselves in the written form.

Men who practice calligraphy are rare. In today's modern world, many women assume that men can't hold a pen because they were brought up using computer and mobile devices. A man with elegant penmanship is sophisticated.

In addition, a calligraphy hobby is a valuable and money-earning skill. People hire calligraphers to create special invitations, memorials, birth/death certificates, diplomas, and more. To learn more about calligraphy, visit www.learncalligraphy.co.uk.

Conjuring / Magic

Conjurer:

Astound your friends with amazing prestidigitation (that's sleight of hand, if you didn't know).

The difference between a conjurer and magician is somewhat blurred. It used to be that a conjurer was thought to cast spells and call up spirits of the dead. These days it's mostly associated with card tricks and pulling rabbits out of the hat. Be careful with conjuring, however, because it's still possible to conjure dark and mischievous spirits (maybe). Classic conjuring texts like "Key of Solomon" are detailed accounts of how to conjure spirits to do your bidding.

The Conjuring Arts Research Center classics, "Magic as a Hobby," (1948) and "Classic Secrets of Magic" (1948) can help you get started with tarot, cartomancy, and other "slick tricks." Visit the Conjuring Arts Research Center at http://conjuringarts.org/ or learn a few simple card tricks here:

http://www.goodtricks.net/cardmagic.html.

Magician:
How many men can float over the Grand Canyon, make the Statue of Liberty disappear and walk through the Great Wall of China? Master magician David Copperfield can.

I'm not suggesting you aspire to such grand illusions, but you can certainly learn to amaze and mystify an audience, even if it is just your grandmother.

Becoming a magician is an exciting hobby for many men. According to the Society of American Magicians, at least 70 percent of magicians are male. The average magician pursues magic as a hobby but say it's possible to secure paid work with some effort. Advertising your services through the society or attending the S.A.M. National Convention for networking purposes can help.

To learn more about magic as a hobby, visit the Society of American Magicians at www.magicsam.com or read the SAM magazine, M-U-M. New magicians may request a free copy. Local magic clubs are often part of IBM as "rings." Contact the International Brotherhood of Magicians via the website at www.magician.org.

Languages

There are about 7,000 languages in the world. Any new language is a good choice for a language learning hobby. If you want to read the great literary works, learn French, Russian, German, or Spanish. If you'd like to visit a new country and want to speak the language (a must if you don't want to be perceived as an arrogant English speaker), then choosing the language of the place you want to visit is the right choice.

Some languages can introduce you to a new way of thinking. For instance, a tribal African language, American Indian language, or Polynesian language can open your mind.

Looking for something more sexy? Try one of the Romance languages: French, Italian or Spanish. Or impress your significant other, "Do you know that the Cherokee language has a single word for the concept of beautiful?"

It's possible to learn the basics of almost any language from your computer these days. Other language courses, like www.RocketLanguages.com, provide instruction for free. Before investing, check out the resources of your public library.

Rocks and fossils

These are the stuff of a fascinating hobby that some call rock-hounding. Collecting rocks—and the fossils sometimes found when exploring rocks—is a lifelong pursuit. Rocks and fossils open doors to the past and can help you understand the creation of earth and its ancient creatures. Here's a useful free download to get you started: http://pubs.usgs.gov/gip/7000011/report.pdf.

Since collecting rocks and fossils can require lots of walking and digging, it's possible to get a workout without going to the gym. Note: If you can't dig the rocks or fossils you've identified, make sure to take pictures of them; keep a precise record of the location in case you or another person needs to return to it.

If you're interested in rocks and fossils as a hobby, learn more at:

- Bureau of Land Management sites
- Rock hobby clubs: Search for a rock hobby club by location.

Rubix

Here's a hobby that some say can became an obsession. Once you crack the 4x4x4, it's clear there are more levels to discover—and 9 and 11-layers cubes! The rubix cube continues to unfold itself to the player and, each time you think you're done, there is more—like the dodecahedral puzzles to solve. If you're bored with the usual three dimensions, it's possible to step up to four
(http://www.superliminal.com/cube/cube.htm)
or even five dimensions
(http://www.gravitation3d.com/magiccube5d/)

Traveling

The days of the intrepid explorer are pretty much gone. None-the-less, if you fancy yourself as a modern day Leif Erikson – a manly man if ever there was – travel adventures can still be had.

Take a look at http://www.incredible-adventures.com/. They'll help you flex your macho muscle diving with big sharks or flying a MiG over Moscow. Cox and Kings will take you on a Himalayan helicopter safari. New Zealand based Thrillseekers will take you on a "stuntcation" where you might even be set on fire.

For the man who wants to get in touch with his wild side, a trip to the Serengeti in Tanzania will get you up-close and personal with lions, wildebeests and crocodiles. And skip the Grand Canyon, go straight to Copper Canyon, Mexico; it's seven times bigger. Then there's Bhutan, a small and somewhat mysterious country in the High Himalayas. Until the 1960s the only way in was on foot and travel is still very much restricted. But if you go, you'll be rewarded with incredible landscapes and an amazing culture and cuisine.

All the trips I've mentioned will cost you a fair bit, but the good news is travel can conform to both your price and comfort level. If you're physically fit, it's possible to bike or hike while you're traveling. If you're interested in soaking up the local flavor or want to save money on food and lodging, it's also possible to rent a home or apartment for a short period.

Take a look at these sites to find out more about traveling:
- Consumer Reports Travel & Vacation Guide at www.consumerreports.org/cro/money/travel-and-vacation-guide/index.htm
- Consumer Affairs: Reviews at https://www.consumeraffairs.com/travel/

Writing

It's hard to say what makes a writer manly. For me it's the tough whisky-drinking, cigar-smoking guys like Mark Twain and Ernest Hemmingway whose writing could bring you to tears. Whatever your thoughts, the key to becoming a good writer is to write – every day.

Start by writing down observations of things that interest you. If you're a gardener, for instance, write about your garden — describe how you raised plants from seeds in February or how you prepared the soil for planting in late spring. You should also read a lot; read the sort of thing you would like to write.

There are different flavors of writing. If you're a university student, you're an academic writer now. If your goal is to write non-fiction books, for instance, you might not find the transition from academic writing that big a stretch.

If you want to write for the Internet or become a blogger, you'll need specific skills to get started. Some schools offer courses in how to write for the web. Whether you take a course or not, you'll need to understand concepts like keywords. There are plenty of good free courses on the topic. HubSpot Academy (academy.hubspot.com) is one to check out.

If you're interested in creative writing, you can take free online courses at Harvard Open Learning at https://www.extension.harvard.edu/open-learning-initiative.

Physical

Blacksmithing

Dating from 1500 BC blacksmithing is the art of forging (shaping) heated iron or steel with hand tools or forging machines. You will need a forge where you keep your fire, bellows or fan and a passageway for the air; anvil and sundry equipment like hammers, chisels, hardies and fullers.

This is a craft that is hot, dirty and physical, which definitely makes it manly in my book. I highly recommend you find a master blacksmith with whom you can train. The ultimate rewards of blacksmithing are that you will acquire the skills to create items that are functional and/or artistic and may even be able to turn your hobby into a profitable business.

Much of what you need to know about blacksmithing can be found online at The Artist Blacksmith's Association of North America site, http://www.abana.org/.

Boxing

The ancient Greeks believed boxing was a sport of the gods, so they humanized it when they included it in the Olympic games around 688 BC. You might think this makes it one of the most manly sports of all. At any rate, along with kickboxing it's become more popular in the past decade. More than six million people participated in boxing in 2014, up more than 50 percent since 2006.

According to ESPN and the NBC Sports Network, boxing is the fastest growing sport for men. Most new boxers are less than 30 years old but more men 30 years and older are boxing for the first time. A growing audience of men who watch boxing contests may be enticing more people to try the sport.

Boxing offers a range of health benefits to men in search of fitness opportunities, including improvements in:
- Muscle tone
- Core stability
- Cardiovascular fitness

- Fat burning (it's possible to burn more than 500 calories in a single session—comparable to a long run)
- Bone/ligament strength
- Muscularity
- Stress reduction

The ESPN Degree of Difficulty Project says that boxing is actually the most difficult to master. It can challenge fit men to acquire new athletic prowess, so it's especially popular with men who want to "reach the next level." To learn more about amateur boxing in the U.S., contact USABF (USA Boxing Foundation), https://boxingfoundation.org/ or search for local private boxing clubs or training facilities.

Fencing

Forget Errol Flynn; this is not the stuff of movies. Fencing is as much art as it is corporeal, the first recorded fight going back to Achilles and Hector in Homer's The Iliad. Today, you would be in company of celebrities such as Tom Cruise, Will Smith and David Beckham.

One of the Historical European Martial Arts (HEMA), according to the U.S. Fencing Organization men represent more than 60 percent of fencers. Experienced fencers get scholarships from some of the best colleges and universities as well. You can find more information about college fencing and college scholarship opportunities at www.scholarshipstats.com/fencing.html.

Fencing also offers significant health benefits, including improved absolute and relative strength and Vo2 max improvements (a measurement of the oxygen used by an athlete). In addition, fencing improves:
- Endurance
- Aerobic and anaerobic fitness levels
- Agility and alertness
- Mental "quickness"
- Flexibility
- Balance and coordination
- Cardiovascular health

Participants typically use replica swords in practice (e.g. saber, foil, and epee) and wear protective facial masks, jackets, and gloves. It can be an expensive hobby, and according to retail statistics, enthusiasts spend billions of dollars each year.

The FIE (Federation Internationale d'Escrime) oversees Olympic Fencing. For reasons unclear, fewer athletes are competing in Olympic fencing today than in the past.

To find out more about fencing, or to find a fencing club, visit the US Fencing website at:
www.usfencing.org/find-a-club

Horses

Whether you just want to ride out on the plains or participate in drill, polo, or equestrian eventing, to some extent you're putting your life into the hooves of a 1200-

pound animal. On the other hand, your horse depends on you to give the right signals and guide him safely through any obstacles.

Owning a horse is a big commitment. Basic care involves feeding (a 1000-pound horse will eat 20 pounds of hay a day), shelter, exercise, grooming, health care and a secure paddock or pasture in which to roam. If you don't have your own stabling facility you will have to board your beast, and you will need the money to cover all these expenses, including equipment such as saddle, bits, bridles, lead ropes, buckets and grooming tools.

If none of that scares you off, and you still espouse the words of John Lubbock, "There is nothing so good for the inside of a man as the outside of a horse." "Recreation," The Use of Life, 1894, then "Hi-yo Silver! Away!"

To learn more about horses and hobbies to enjoy horses, contact:
- The United States Equestrian Drill Association at useda.homestead.com/
- The United States Polo Association on facebook: https://www.facebook.com/USPoloAssociation
- The United States Eventing Association at www.useventing.com

Martial arts & Mixed martial arts

Enthusiasts these days typically train in mixed martial arts. However, some learn traditional martial arts

(TMA) first, which are bound in the principles of the original master of the art. Some of the more well-known styles of TMA are Aikido, Judo, Jujitsu, Karate, Kendo, Kung Fu and Sumo. Experts say there's no way to easily answer which style is best.

Mixed martial arts incorporates and encourages the use of various fighting styles in a competition. It's become more popular since the rollout of the UFC "Ultimate Fighting Championship."

Although MMA is more accepting of fight moves than TMA, there are some moves that are simply forbidden any time. There's no eye-gouging, hair-pulling, head-butting, etc. Elbow strikes may be allowed in some places and optional rules may apply.

Claiming victory in MMA includes: 1) knock-out; 2) submission; 3) scoring; 4) forfeit; 5) disqualification; and 6) no contest. For example, a MMA competitor forfeits when he pulls out of the match before it begins.

There's no simple way to learn MMA. Many people complain it's almost impossible to find one trainer to teach you everything. It's up to you to chart the course.

If you're already an advanced traditional martial artist, MMA may be the way to take your skills to the next level. It can enhance the functionality of your fighting style.

To learn more about martial arts, visit the United States Martial Arts Association at www.wwmaa.org, the Universal Martial Arts Association at www.universal-martial-arts.org, or the International Martial Arts Council at www.imacusa.com/.

Rowing

Does anyone remember the TV show Banacek? George Peppard played a detective and the opening credits always showed him rowing on the Charles River in Boston in the very early morning. It was a compelling shot and always made me want to learn to row.

Rowing requires a combination of strength, endurance and technique. Shells (boats) are built for one or up to eight rowers. A single athlete, with two oars, is a sculler. Pairs of two to eight rowers have one oar each and are known as sweep rowers. All rowers face backwards except the coxswain – if they have one – who steers the boat and coaxes the team on.

Colleges perhaps have the preponderance of rowing clubs but there are others dotted around so search your area. Online, look at US Rowing, http://www.usrowing.org.

Skydiving

Another male-dominated hobby. Let's be honest, it takes some cojones to hurl yourself from a perfectly good airplane into vast nothingness 13,000 feet or more above solid ground.

According to the United States Parachute Association (USPA), about 86 percent of skydivers are male. About fifty percent of skydivers are between the ages of 16 and 39. About 10 percent of skydivers are 60 years or older. Most skydivers are active, participating in hundreds of dives over the years.

Before making a first dive, it's necessary to train for the event. Since about 500,000 people try skydiving each year in the U.S., selecting a drop zone school is the first step. The new skydiver must pass first-jump courses using USPA-approved equipment. [Note: the USPA is FAA-approved]

After about four to five hours of training, most people are ready to make a first skydive. Although it's possible to start with a USPA online school, these courses aren't considered sufficient training for a first jump.

Skydiving is an expensive hobby:

- An average tandem skydive costs about $200 in the U.S. Those skydiving with a group may benefit from group rates.
- Accelerated Free Fall (AFF) is typically more expensive. Training for AFF can cost thousands. In order to earn a dive license (to dive without supervision), most students must dive an average 25 times at more than $200 per dive.
- It's possible to rent skydiving gear but, for those who want their own, plan to spend $5000 to $9000 for main/reserve canopies, helmet, altimeter, and goggles.

In addition to allowing the skydiver to conquer fear or experience the thrill of freefall, skydiving's health benefits include improved strength and development of arm and lower body muscle groups. Many skydivers say that skydiving offers unparalleled stress relief. Facing fears and taking a big leap creates confidence.

To learn more about skydiving, contact the USPA at www.uspa.org.

Sports coach

Say yes if you're asked to coach a sport. It's a great avocation and a way to catch up with friends and find out what's going on in the community as you play a role in encouraging young people.

Coaching is all about helping each player succeed. As a coach, you can help children understand that life is a team sport, too.

Visit the National Youth Sports Coaches Association – National Alliance for Youth Sports at https://www.nays.org/coaches or the Positive Coaching Alliance (PCA) at www.positivecoach.org.

Wingsuit flying

Picture this. You jump from a small plane or the top of a sheer rock face, spread your arms and legs, stretching your nylon jumpsuit so you become a single wing, and soar through the air at breath-taking speed.

Wingsuit flying is an extreme skydiving sport that makes use of a special jumpsuit called a wingsuit, birdman suit, or squirrel suit. There are two arm "wings" and a single leg wing on the wingsuit, which increase the wingsuit flyer's surface area to allow him or her the ability to fly horizontal distances at slowed descent rates. In other words, the wingsuit flyer wants to increase freefall time.

Wingsuit flying requires the flyer to use the body to control lift, direction, and forward speeds. These skills are not learned in a day—it may require years to achieve desired efficient wingflight or management of the wingsuit. Performance is measured with GPS devices and by flying with others to determine relative speeds and distances. This grouping together is called flocking.

Hobbies for Men

Read the America's Best Adventures page "Learn to Fly a Wingsuit" at:
adventure.nationalgeographic.com/adventure/trips/Americas-best-adventures/wingsuit-flying/ or visit the World Wingsuit League at worldwingsuitleague.com for more information.

Wrestling

"More enduringly than any other sport, wrestling teaches self-control and pride. Some have wrestled without great skill – none have wrestled without pride." ~ Dan Gable

Anyone remember the British actor Oliver Reed? He was known for his macho image and hellraiser lifestyle. In a scene from a 1969 movie, Women in Love, he wrestled Alan Bates. The thing that made it memorable – both men were naked. At the time it practically rocked the British Empire (I might be exaggerating a little here), but here's the thing, as erotic as it was, hardly anyone thought it was anything other than intensely masculine – especially the ladies.

Now, wrestling may not give you quite the same image these days, but pitting brute strength, balance and cunning against an equally skilled opponent is certainly a manly thing. But if mano-a-mano doesn't appeal to you, consider watching pro wrestling instead.

There are several wrestling organizations in the U.S., including World Wrestling Entertainment (because some of the best known wrestlers are entertainers), Total

D.L. Haley

Nonstop Action (TNA), and the Ring of Honor (ROH). To learn more about regional wrestling associations, visit:
   http://www.regionwrestlingacademy.com/ and themat.com.

Social

Amateur theatrics

Make your dreams of acting—or set design or costuming—come true. You could find yourself playing the part of macho Terry Malloy in *On the Waterfront*, or hey, maybe a villainous Iago in Shakespeare's *Othello*.

Amateur theatre groups are almost everywhere. If you're hoping to act or sing, an amateur theatre group near you is bringing stage plays, variety shows, light opera, musicals, and so much more to theatregoers.

Amateur theatrics may be called "community theatre." According to the American Association of Community Theatre, there are almost 1,000 member organizations that offer amateur theatrics opportunities to the public. Although community theatre members generally don't draw a paycheck, it's possible (under Actors' Equity association) for a community theatre to pay up to two "guest performers."

To learn more about amateur theatrics, visit the American Association of Community Theatre at www.aact.org or search for U.S. community theatres in your area. For international amateur theatrics, visit the International Amateur Theatre Association (AITA/IATA) at http://www.aitaiata.org/gil/

If you're interested in performing in this kind of venue, consider preparing a resume and photo to share with community theatres about yourself.

Ballroom dancing

Before *Dancing With the Stars* I know a lot of you thought that gliding across the dance floor was for sissies. Well let me tell you, it requires stamina, grace, confidence, patience, and it doesn't hurt to have some natural rhythm. You will also be mentally challenged to remember all the steps and to lead your lady. That's right guys. Ballroom dancing is actually one of the most manly hobbies you can do because you are in charge. The lady always follows your lead. And let me tell you, there is a surplus of women who would dearly like to find a man who can dance. If you're already happily enchained, um, in a relationship, then your partner will likely be thrilled if you start dancing.

There are many dance schools so look around your local area. It's absolutely OK to go solo. You'll be put in the capable hands of a female instructor and most schools have regular dance nights for their students where you will find yourself in high demand regardless of your skill level.

The cost for lessons is very varied. As a general rule, count on paying $400 to $500 for a package of about a dozen private and group lessons at one of the well-known schools. For something a little cheaper look for local community groups that offer classes.

Big Brother

Yes, become a Big Brother. By volunteering for just a few hours a month you can help to shape a child's future for the better. Now, that's what I call manly.

There are thousands of kids right now waiting to be matched with a Big Brother. You can play sports together, visit museums or the movies, or simply listen and talk. Or, hey! Here's a novel idea, you could start a hobby together – like astronomy or beekeeping.

Find out everything you need to know at the Big Brothers Big Sisters website: http://www.bbbs.org.

Board games

Board games are experiencing a renaissance as more app versions of class board games reach our mobile devices. Mary Pilon, an author (The Monopolists) and journalist, theorizes that physical board games bring people together and allow them to unplug from technology. There's a trend among techies to return digital games to the tactile and cardboard world. To learn more about board game groups, search www.meetup.com for a techie board game group near you.

D.L. Haley

Campanology

Most people I mention this to think it's something to do with the methodology of setting up a camp. Wrong! Campanology is Change Ringing and, for those of you who are still confused, we're talking about Bell Ringing, where a group of people ring the bells through changing sequences. Strictly speaking, hand bells come under the heading of change ringing, but I'm just referring to the type of large bells (100 to 3600 pounds in weight) that you find in church and school towers.

The balanced bells are attached to large vertical wheels and rung by pulling on ropes that run around the wheel's rim. It sounds easy but, as a former campanologist I can tell you that it requires a careful touch and can be dangerous. If a ringer loses control the rope will whip around wildly and can cause serious injury.

Change Ringing is an old art, going back to the 1600s and requires both physical and mental stamina. Methods – the changes in the order in which the bells are rung – can go on for hours. Often, the changes will be called out by a conductor but there are times when you may be required to memorize them.

England is by far the center of bell-ringing but there are active towers in Australia and New Zealand. And for those of you in the USA, go to the North American Guild of Change Ringers to find out more. http://www.nagcr.org/.

Civil War reenactor

Friends of mine were Civil War sutler (provisioner) reenactors, and I got to see first-hand how dedicated (I could say crazy) some of these guys are. In 20-degree, snowy weather, they would sleep amongst the trees with only a thin woolen blanket for cover, in order to be true to their hobby. That's just a bit too manly for me.

Reenacting allows you to bring history to life as a living historian. If you've read about the Civil War — and you've committed some of the battles to memory — Civil War reenacting can be a fulfilling next step.

D.L. Haley

Similarly, if your passion is any genre of Medieval history or World War II, it's possible to join with others and reenact a battle of choice wearing realistic garb of the day.
- Civil War reenactors were first recognized at "The Great Reunion of 1913," a memorialization of the Battle of Gettysburg's 50th anniversary. The Great Reunion drew tens of thousands of original Confederate and Union vets together to reenact the battle.
- Since the 1960s, modern reenactors have got together to commemorate the Civil War.
- After the reenactment of the 125th anniversary of the Battle of Manassas (which drew thousands of reenactors), reenacting has continued to grow. A reenactment of the Battle of Gettysburg (135th anniversary) attracted about 20,000 reenactors and thousands of spectators.

It's possible to participate in reenactments of major wars around the world. For instance, the American Civil War Society is a group of reenactors in the UK.

Contact the Civil War Reenactment Society, www.cwrs.info/Civil_War_Reenactment_Society/Home.html), or living history group that appeals to you to get started.

Darts

Darts is a hobby that combines well with social or solo circumstances, and lots of beer drinking. At least, in my experience beer always seems to play a part.

Quite likely you know darts originated in England, and it's said even Henry VIII enjoyed a game. Now there was a man; I'll bet he liked a few beers too. And it's believed the pilgrims entertained themselves with a game of darts now and then on their voyage to America aboard the Mayflower. In other words, darts has been a game of men for centuries.

You might think anyone can throw a dart. True enough, but it doesn't mean they can consistently hit on the board where they need to. For that, you have to develop the right throwing technique, which requires many hours of practice.

Darts and dartboards are relatively inexpensive, and this is as competitive a hobby as you'd like it to be. Learn more about competitive darts at the World Darts Federation site at www.dartswdf.com or the American Darts Organization at www.adodarts.com.

Ham radio

Also known as amateur radio, ham radio is a non-internet or cell phone/mobile device method of communication. It's old school. People use amateur radio to talk with other ham radio operators around the world or across the street. Ham radio operators boast that they can always communicate. Unlike cell phones and devices that crash in a power outage, the ham operator can reach other operators on FCC amateur bands, or radio frequencies assigned to amateur radio operators.

D.L. Haley

According to the American Radio Relay League (ARRL), ham operators use Morse Code or voice communications via hand-held radio or transmitted from a computer via satellite. The FCC allows ham operators to communicate because, in the event of communication emergency, these people can "get the word out." Ham operators work in crisis situations, such as earthquakes or hurricane conditions, to help the communities and regions they live in.

Visit www.arrl.org for more information about ham radio.

Larping

Larping, or live action role-playing (LARP), allows players to act out characters' goals in a fictional world, while they're in the real world. As the description suggestions, larping is like playing a role-playing computer game with real people who assume the characters of the game.

Larping is another example of how humans want to bring ideas and imaginary worlds into the physical realm. We're hard-wired to use our physical, visual, tactile, olfactory, and as yet unexplained senses. From the manly standpoint, this adult version of make-believe often seems to revolve around battles and weapons.

If you're improvisational, or you like the idea of improvising and/or amateur theatre, larping can be an exciting and fun hobby. Read more about larping at http://www.larping.org.

Podcaster

If you enjoy sharing your thoughts and opinions with others online, you might enjoy a podcaster hobby. Podcasting isn't new — it's been around for a little more than a decade — so you can choose a short podcast about any subject that interests you (politics, history, or science, for example). After you build a group of followers, your podcasts can be downloaded and enjoyed by others for many years in the future.

Some podcasts have been watched as often as the most popular tv shows. If podcasting interests you, it's one way to share your knowledge (e.g. the "Stuff You Should Know" podcasts) or give good advice (e.g. "Planet Money") to people who need it. Some podcasts have a host and guests, like Freakanomics Radio, The Nerdist, or The Dave Ramsey Show.

Becoming a podcaster requires attention to detail and lots of time. That's why, if you're good at podcasting, it might be a great next career for you.

To learn more about podcasting, visit the International Association of Internet Broadcasters (IAIB) at www.ibroadcastnetwork.org.

D.L. Haley

Pool

Depending upon your level of interest or skill, playing pool or billiards is considered a challenging or relaxing hobby, and a decent pool table can be had for well under $1,000.

Acquiring pool shooting skills isn't easy. If you want to be good at pool, plan to work at your skills over a life time. There are many online videos that show the basics of pool and billiards so study a few and practice, practice, practice.

If you're interested in playing in a pool tournament, you'll want to practice the game using standard equipment. Not all tables conform to World Pool-Billiards Association dimensions.

Believe it or not, you can also play online billiards. You use a mouse to navigate the virtual cue stick for money. If you like the idea of playing online, limit the amount of money you're willing to lose.

You can get inspiration from members of the Billiard Hall of Fame. Players like Ralph Greenleaf, Willie Hoppe (who won 50 or more world titles), John Wesley Hyatt, or "The Miz" (Steve Mizerak) show it's possible to earn fame and fortune playing pool or billiards.

Learn more about pool and billiards at the Billiard Congress of America at www.bca-pool.com.

Public speaking

It takes a real man to get up on a podium and give a speech. I can say that because it terrifies me.

Public speaking can boost confidence and self-esteem, can provide an effective platform to promote new ideas and offers an opportunity to meet new professional and social contacts. Even better, you may be able to turn your talent into paid speaking engagements.

Think you have nothing to talk about? Of course you do. You can talk about any other hobbies and interests you have. Your business experience could be a source of interest for others. How about family or personal struggles? I once met an author who began by giving free presentations about struggling to get published (this was in the days before self-publishing); these days he gets five-figures for a two-hour speech.

Start at Toastmasters:

http://www.toastmasters.org/ or look around your local area for other speaking clubs.

Poker

Poker is possibly the king of card games and top tournament players can earn millions. Of course, you can just play for the fun of it. Either way, it's a manly game and, as many popular movies attest, it's a feast or famine game for some who play poker for money. (Anyone seen The Cincinnati Kid, with Steve McQueen?)

Learning how to play poker well requires the ability to keep a poker face. You mustn't let your face or mannerisms convey your hand to others. And there are some really masculine poker sets you can buy, like one from Man Crates that comes in a .30 caliber ammo can. Or check ebay for a classic set in a wood or leather case.

Playing poker with friends or with a local poker club is one of the best ways to learn poker. Online sites come and go — you may have noticed there were hundreds of poker sites online a few years ago. Today, there are hundreds to thousands of poker apps for your mobile phone. Before playing poker online, know that the house advantage is real. Don't bet money you need for life's essentials.

To learn more about poker, visit Poker Players Alliance at https://www.theppa.org or search for "poker club" near you.

Creative

Carpentry

For thousands of years civilizations have used wood to create objects of use and beauty. Just look at China's Nanchan Temple, the oldest wooden structure standing. It's not known when it was first built, but it was rebuilt during the Tang Dynasty (AD 782).

If you love fine furnishings, you're probably aware that carpentry (especially old school knowledge) has made a comeback. Restoration carpenters, or carpenters making fine furniture from hand a la 17th, 18th, and 19th centuries, are making tons of money.

The word carpentry comes from the French, charpentier, which means carriage maker. It is a highly skilled trade, but learning the hands-on art of old school carpentry is possible without the advantage of a master carpenter at your side. Fine Woodworking Magazine (http://www.finewoodworking.com/) has projects and step-by-step information about how to make the kind of furniture most people wish they had in their homes these days. If you're a fine carpentry hobbyist, your skills are highly marketable.

D.L. Haley

Cooking

There are so many reasons why cooking is a great hobby. It makes you more independent, you'll probably eat better than you do now, you can impress and treat others, it's a great way to socialize and women love a guy who can cook. Even James Bond can cook a quiche (*A View To A Kill*) so there goes that real man myth. In fact, any life skill is manly. If you can hunt and build a fire, shouldn't you know how to cook?

There are several ways to go about this. Get someone to teach you the basics or take local classes. If you're like me, you'll just teach yourself. When I left home (my mother was a great cook) I couldn't afford anything close to fine dining and I really missed that home cooking. So I figured if I could read and I could reason then I ought to be able to follow a recipe. I've been preparing meals since then. In fact, I do most of the cooking in my home.

For those of you who are really ambitious, once you're comfortable with the basics you might even consider The Escoffier Online International Culinary Academy. They offer a self-paced virtual culinary program that is a fraction of the price of going to school. Auguste Escoffier, of course, was a legendary French chef who popularized French cooking methods and elevated cooking to the status of respected profession. (Ah, another manly man). Take a look at the courses here: http://www.escoffieronline.com.

Drumming

This is not the drumming of Alex Van Halen or Phil Collins, though that's certainly a great hobby, and skill, to have. I'm talking about hand drumming.

Almost anyone can learn drumming—you don't need to read music or have a background in music theory, you actually don't even need drums. Drumming is almost a universal language because almost every culture in the world has drumming of some sort in its tradition.

The act of drumming is proven to reduce stress. According to Dr. Ann Webster, drumming can send the drummer into a meditative state and reduce the drummer's blood pressure. Adding deep breathing to drumming can make it even more relaxing. Cancer expert

Dr. Barry Bitman says research shows that group drumming will promote cancer-fighting cells.

Many shamanic traditions include drumming because the act of drumming increases synchrony of the brain hemispheres and increased alpha waves. Drumming is a simple and powerful way to express the self.

Search for free drumming courses online or search for a local drumming teacher on sites like Yelp. To learn more about the health benefits of drumming, visit www.DrumStrong.org.

Duct tape art

This isn't just a popular craft hobby, it's a cultural phenomenon. The New York Daily News says it's possible to use duct tape to make useful or eye-catching items. A long-lived scholarship program, "Stuck at Prom," encourages creative high school students to turn duct tape into a prom dress or tuxedo. Manly men have created everything from a batman mask, backpack, hammock and snowshoes to a boat with a fishing net.

Duct tape art is inexpensive. To make a bag, you'll need about 20 yards of tape. At three to five dollars a roll, it's possible to express yourself on a budget.

To learn more, read Richela Fabian Morgan's "Tape It and Make It," or "Tape It and Make More." (2014) You can also find lots of instructional videos on YouTube: search for YouTube duct tape art to begin.

Glass blowing

Evidence of glass blowing dates back to the 16th century B.C. in Mesopotamia and ancient glassforming techniques were closely guarded, traditionally handed down from experienced glassblowers to apprentices of the art.

Creative artists and designers show renewed interest in glassblowing today. A blob of red-hot molten glass is shaped by puffing air through a pipe to expand it, then using various tools to shape the glass. The process requires creative vision, manual dexterity and a fair degree of stamina.

Artist communities, such as the Torch Life Glass Artist Community, train new glassblowers. Visit the Torch Life website at www.torchlife.us/training.cfm.

Handmade crafts and art

Creating individual and functional items can be very satisfying for men who spend much of their time in the technological world, and the analog process helps release the stresses that a complex workday brings.

Candle making may not seem very manly, but how about bacon candles? As an extra benefit, you get to eat the bacon. Making things out of old vinyl records is cool, but don't use collectible ones. Repurpose old wood to make hammock stands. There's tons of stuff you can make out of old wine corks. And while we're on the subject of booze...Beer bikes! Really! Not only is this artsy, craftsy and manly, you can make money with it. Take a look: http://www.trendhunter.com/trends/the-beer-bike.

Home brewing

According to the American Homebrewers Associations, http://www.homebrewersassociation.org more than 1 million enthusiasts in the USA brew beer at home. Their site is a great resource for the beginner brewer with brewing instructions, recommended reading and links to find local clubs.

Man discovered the potential for converting grain into alcohol even before the written language. The first known description of brewing dates back to 3800 BC. In ancient Babylon, laws were written for tavern owners selling beer. In other words, throughout history beer has been an important part of man's diet and lifestyle.

To begin your first batch of beer you can get a starter kit for less than $100. This will include something like this:

    Instructions
    5-gallon glass carboy
    6.5-gallon plastic fermenter with lid
    6.5-gallon bottling bucket with spigot
    4-oz. of Easy Clean No-Rinse Cleanser
    Drilled universal carboy bung
    Airlock (Keeps air out of the fermenter)

Hydrometer (Determines alcohol content)
Bottle brush
Carboy brush
Twin Lever Bottle Capper
Bottle caps
Liquid crystal thermometer
Bottle filler
Siphon tubing
Shutoff clamp

You will also need a brewpot and bottles and, of course, ingredients, which can also be purchased in kit form and will cost up to $45 for a 5 gallon batch depending on the style of brew. This should net you 48 12-ounce bottles within a month or so and after just a few hours work.

Home brewing will save you money in the long run. You'll have pride in your accomplishment and, in time, you might develop your own personalized recipes. You won't be able to sell your home brew though you can certainly gift a few bottles to friends and family, and before embarking on a brewing bash, check your local laws to be sure you conform with all the legalities of this craft and have any necessary permits.

D.L. Haley

Leatherworking (also called Leather Crafting)

Leather has been an essential part of man's evolution. It has provided shelter and clothing, been used as currency and for writing on, has been tooled into a myriad articles – horse gear, jewelry, pitchers, helmets, drums, furniture covering.

From basic bookmarks to intricate bags and even armor, crafting items from leather can provide hours of creative enjoyment and even become a money-making proposition. Get yourself a solid work bench. Yes, for simple objects it's possible to practice your craft in the living room in front of the TV but you'll be using some very sharp tools so it's much better to focus all your attention on leatherworking and use safe practices.

For less than $40 you can buy a basic tool set from places such as Tandy Leather Factory, http://www.tandyleatherfactory.com. Then you'll need a leather craft mallet at around $10 and of course, the leather. Leather is sometimes sold by the square foot, or buy a side of Kodiak leather, perfect for gear that will be exposed to the elements, for about $200. Whole rabbit skins will run about $10 and hair-on cowhides (about 5 foot by 6 foot) might run up to $200 or more.

Most leathers will require moisture to soften them before working, then you can use stamps to create designs in the skin. Next a special finish is sponged on to the leather to enhance and protect it. Now you will stitch your item together and add any snaps or rivets that are needed.

For more information browse around the Tandy site and also look at Leatherworker, http://leatherworker.net/ where they have a fairly active forum.

Model ship building

Whatever else, start with a model ship kit, do not try and build from scratch – yet. Even some of the kits can be quite complex and you might end up abandoning the project in frustration, which is not at all manly. It takes a lot of tools to put together a model, so I recommend that you get a kit package that includes tools and paint. For an entry level model with tools expect to pay $200 or so.

This hobby is for the man who enjoys detailed hand work and can be very patient. The rewards are great when you are able to sit back and admire your own recreation of seafaring history. Another facet to model ship building is restoration of antique models. Over the years I've come across a number of sad-looking but once proud model ships and never risen to the occasion. I regret that now.

Anyway, begin your new hobby at Model Ship World, http://modelshipworld.com/, a forum for every level of ship modeler and a great resource for tips and techniques. To buy models your best selection will be online using a google search.

Musical instruments

Something else for people who crave the opportunity to get away from the technical world now and then. Musical instruments, especially unusual musical instruments like the banjo or bagpipes, combine the tactile sense some guys crave with the bone-stimulating sound of music. Creating music for personal expression and enjoyment helps to unplug the individual attached to an iPhone or keyboard during the work day. Reports suggest that using the hands to perform something without a work-related purpose can make you happy. Make some music to break up a high pressure 90-hour week at work.

Here's a comprehensive list of musical instruments, some with sound files, to help you choose. Personally, I like the balalaika. https://www.imit.org.uk/pages/a-to-z-of-musical-instrument.html.

Photography and Lomography

Today's photography favors digital tools instead of time-honored photographic film. In contrast, lomography is an artistic movement that encourages the use of film instead of LCD screens. Many men report an "addiction" to shooting analog photos.

According to NPR, most lomographers are between the ages of 18 and 28. A TIME Magazine poll reports that most lomographers are comfortable with digital and communication technology. Almost half listen to vinyl records in addition to digital music. More than half keep paper photograph albums of lomograph (analog) photos. Most own classic analog cameras and have developed their films and prepared printed photos in a darkroom.

The reasons lomographers use film makes sense. For instance, medium format film can potentially capture 400 MP when compared to digital scans capturing a mere 50-80 MP resolution. In addition, large formats, e.g. four by five inches, potentially capture 200 MP photos after scanning. Consider that an old 35 mm camera can't compete with a current digital camera—but a specialized medium or large format camera can exceed the resolution of our latest $30-60,000 Phase One units. This fact alone can make lomography an attractive and less costly hobby.

D.L. Haley

According to American Photography, about 40 percent of all photographers offer services part-time. Some hobbyists perform the functions that full time photographers don't. For instance, only about 13 percent of professional wedding photography studios offer wedding videography as a service. Only 13 percent offer catalog services and 14 percent offer pet photos.

According to InfoTrends, part-time photography hobbyists have multiple opportunities to earn money taking pictures of nature, products, architecture, travel, fashion, and more even though competition is brisk.

Photography, videography, and lomography can be an expensive hobby:

- A new digital camera costs a few hundred to thousands of dollars for higher-end models. It's possible to find bargains in high quality film cameras if the hobbyist is willing to look for used equipment.
- Additional equipment, including lenses, flashes, tripods, and cases can be costly but, again, some great bargains are possible if the user is willing to buy items at auction or secondhand.
- Lomographers need film, paper, and a dark room to develop film. The space must be properly ventilated with a safelight (glowing brown or red). The photographer will also need enlargers, filters, and a sink for developing and rinsing film. In addition, chemicals and a development tank, trays, tongs, timers, and more are needed for negatives and finished photos.

- Courses to learn photography techniques can add to the cost of the hobby. Look for courses offered at community colleges to save money on gaining photography expertise.

For more information about photography hobbies, visit regional camera club or photography organization websites. Local clubs and associations can also help hobbyists to make money or gain recognition in photography.

Visit www.lomography.com to learn more about this artistic movement.

Videographers should visit sites like the National Alliance for Media Arts and Culture (NAMAC) at www.namac.org.

Sculpting from junk

You know what they say about one man's trash. Well, here's the perfect example. Floyd Gompf has scavenged other peoples' discards and created crazy good pieces of furniture that sell for as much as $3000 and have made him quite a cult figure. Look online for some of his furniture.

Art has been created from electronic trash, soda cans, kitchen items, coat hangers, computer circuit boards. I've seen a steam iron transposed into a table lamp. Point is, if you're the kind of guy who has a little imagination and likes wielding a blow torch and a hammer, junk sculpting may be your métier.

D.L. Haley

Believe it or not, there are even junk sculpting contests. That means you have a chance to capitalize on your hobby in two ways – prize money and sales of your art.

Silversmithing

Tooled silver artifacts date back to as early as 500 and 600 BC, and this truly ancient craft has changed relatively little since then.

For as little as $200 you can purchase sufficient tools and supplies to begin your hobby. You'll need to set up a work space, which should be in a secure place as you will be working with chemicals, an acetylene torch and other sharp instruments.

The Society of American Silversmiths has a list of recommended reading that I suggest you peruse: http://www.silversmithing.com/books.htm and there are many online silversmithing courses you could check out. However, before jumping in with both feet, how about signing up for a local community class? Your upfront costs will be minimal and you'll have a chance to find out if this is the hobby for you.

That said, guys, this could be more than just a satisfying pastime. Think how impressed the ladies in your life will be when you present them with your own handcrafted gifts. Working with silver could also become another money-maker. A friend of mine who is a coin dealer had a pile of old silver coins that were so worn they no longer had any numismatic value. He melted them down and crafted them into rings that he sold for $70 each. He reckoned his cost was $3 to $5 per ring, plus his time. Not a bad profit.

Whittling

Time was that almost every man (and boy) used to carry a pocket knife and could be ready to turn a piece of wood into a work of rustic art. Now we all carry cell phones and there's nothing about a phone that helps a man center his thoughts or just relax and while away the time. So perhaps it's time to consider whittling.

The only things you need are a good knife – there are specialty whittling knives available but they're fixed blade, which means they're not easily portable – wood and time. Knives can be bought for as little as $20 or you can get whittling kits that also include patterns, wood and instructions. Just take a look on Amazon. And if you don't want to wander in the woods looking for suitable pieces to whittle then softwood blocks can be purchased. Basswood is the most common wood for sale and I saw several good buys on ebay.

There's a good book that you might read, The Little Book of Whittling by Chris Lubkemann. It will teach you everything you need to know and, of course, can be found on Amazon.

This is another hobby that can also turn you a buck or two. In my hallway are a walking cane and hiking stick that were carved by a friend. Canes are all he whittles. He began by just giving sticks away, then more and more people started to ask if he would make canes for them for a fee. He doesn't make much, but he covers his expenses and gets to escort a lovely lady to dinner once in a while.

Outdoors

Archery

The Egyptians, the Assyrians, the Hittites, the Romans, all relied on the bow and arrow for hunting and fighting. Genghis Khan and his Mongol hordes used bows to conquer much of the known world. The bow was the weapon used by William the Conqueror to over-run England. In fact, archery has been practiced since at least 3500 BC and the bow and arrow has probably impacted the world more than any other weapon in history.

A good place to start researching archery is the National Field Archery Association, https://www.nfaausa.com/ where you'll also find links to local associations and whose motto says it all: Archery – The sport of man since time began. Don't rush out to buy equipment 'til you're sure that this is the hobby for you. A decent longbow will cost you about $500.

Backpacking

A perennial favorite for men of all ages. Backpackers enjoy the activity for the health benefits and the opportunity to explore new vistas. Go solo or with a group and imagine yourself as a modern day Daniel

Boone, trailblazing a way to virgin places. While you won't experience the same kind of a rough and dangerous life as ole Dan, you will learn self-reliance and the value of independence.

There are two basic forms of backpacking: camping and traveling. Whether planning a single day hike or week-long hike, more men than ever enjoy trekking for pleasure. According to CNBC, more than 140 million people hike and camp.

Backpacking can be expensive. The cost of packs, emergency blankets, fire starters, headlamps, maps, compass, first-aid kit, sleeping bag, tent, and more can cost the high-tech backpacker thousands of dollars (source: REI).

To learn more about hiking and backpacking, or to find a club, visit www.hikingandbackpacking.com.

Beekeeping

Create some buzz about yourself by setting up a honeybee colony. Bees may always be busy but if your time is limited beekeeping should only require a half hour to one hour of your time each week. You'll need to do a little planning first, though. Check that there are no legal restrictions in your area, and it's a good idea to make sure the neighbors are OK with your potential hobby. And be sure you can provide a safe, natural habitat.

There will be some start-up costs involved. Experts generally recommend a minimum of two hives, Fully-assembled hives can be found for as little as $150 though you can easily pay a lot more. Expect to fork out about $200 for protective clothing and tools. A two to four-pound package of bees (you'll need one for each hive) will run $80 to $100 each. So expect to pay $700 to $1000 to get started.

The good news is that there are few ongoing costs and you might even recoup your money by selling some of your little workers' product. A hive might produce just a few pounds or well over a 100 pounds of raw honey a year that can sell for $10 a pound or more.

There are lots of online resources for beekeeping, including the Old Farmer's Almanac:

http://www.almanac.com/blog/home-health/bees.

Camping

Here's a way for men to reconnect with the natural world. Connecting with nature every so often is essential. Sleeping beneath the moon and stars, cooking at a camp fire or stone, and snuggling with your special someone in a sleeping bag for two is the definition of getting away from work or whatever ails you.

Camping is also one of the least expensive ways to take a vacation. If you've made an investment in a tent—and many of today's tents are amazingly comfortable and inexpensive—you can seek out new vistas whenever you hear the call of the wild.

D.L. Haley

If you enjoy fishing, backpacking, kayaking, canoeing, or whitewater rafting, camping is a must. For more information on how to get started, visit http://camping.about.com/od/campingforbeginners/

Cowboy

Years ago it seemed that every other kid wanted to grow up to be a cowboy. Cowboys were tough but fair, respectful of womenfolk, could toss a coin in the air and shoot a hole through it, were brave but modest. Then the popularity of the western lifestyle faded into the sunset for a time. Well, now it's coming back.

There's more to the cowboy than wearing boots and a Stetson, though clothing is a part of it. You don't need to own a horse but you should know how to handle one, and I don't recommend hitting the rodeo trail except as an observer. Skills like roping and shooting ought to be practiced, and to eat like a cowboy you might try cooking over a camp fire (don't be too picky about what it is), keep your back to the wind so grit doesn't blow onto your plate and eat fast before the food gets cold.

Most importantly, live by the Cowboy Code. The Center for Cowboy Ethics and Leadership promotes the following ten principles to live by:

1. Live each day with courage
2. Take pride in your work
3. Always finish what you start

4. Do what has to be done
5. Be tough, but fair
6. When you make a promise, keep it
7. Ride for the brand
8. Talk less and say more
9. Remember that some things aren't for sale
10. Know where to draw the line.

There's more here:
http://elvaquero.com/cowboy-code/.
So start sleeping under the stars and using cowboy 'figgers' of speech like "You can put yer boots in the oven but that don't make them biscuits" or "That politician is a flannel-mouthed liar" and start riding your own happy trails.

Cycling and mountain biking

Most likely you learned to ride as a kid, but getting back on a bike isn't necessarily as easy as many say. Seriously, have you ever watched the Tour de France or a mountain bike race? For that you've got to be fanatically fit and focused, and maybe just a little bit crazy.

Here's the thing, though. You don't have to be an advanced rider to participate in some pretty manly biking adventures. For instance, there are companies that will take you fatbiking (the bike has over-sized tires) in the Arctic Circle, past glaciers and fiords and through remote wilderness. You just have to be fit and willing to live life to the fullest.

Competitive cyclists are predominantly male (about 87 percent) and between the ages of 35 to 44. A large percentage (about 17 percent) are Californians (go figure) so says USA Cycling research. Western U.S. states seem to grow the most cycling enthusiasts. Cycling and mountain biking are popular with a wide range of men (24 to 62 years). Most new cyclists are at least 30 years old.

The health benefits of cycling and mountain biking are plentiful, including:

- Calorie burning and weight control: Mountain bikers can burn up to 1,000 calories/hour depending on intensity.
- People for Bikes reports that just three hours of cycling per week reduces the chance of developing cardiovascular disease. Cycling just 30 minutes a day reduces breast cancer risk.
- Cycling is a joint-friendly activity. Older Americans, or athletes suffering from over-use injuries, can benefit from cardiovascular benefits and less high impact. (Note: After years as a runner, President George W. Bush embraced mountain biking.)
- Cycling reduces stress. A Kent State University study (2007) says that cycling and mountain biking can reduce stress while providing participants with "adventure" and physical challenges.
- According to the Mayo Clinic, cycling and mountain biking can also promote endorphin release that

defends against depression. Cycling or mountain biking can make participants feel happier.

To learn more about cycling and mountain biking, visit International Mountain Bicycling Organization at https://www.imba.com or the USA Cycling website at www.usacycling.org.

Falconry

Ah, the 'sport of kings' and definitely not for the common man. The falconer apprenticeship takes two years and to become a Master Falconer will take at least seven years. Permits and licenses require taking a written falconry exam and, in some states, taking a hunter education course. Then you will have to be inspected before you can even acquire a raptor.

Your hawk (eagle, owl, falcon) will require care 365 days a year, let alone endless patience when training. You'll need money – a lot – for food, mandated housing, veterinary care, permits, equipment, travel, training. And you may have to face animal rights activists who disapprove of falconry.

This is just the beginning. And after you've invested all the time, money and effort there's always the possibility that your raptor will take a free flight, literally, and soar away never to be seen again.

If you still think falconry might be for you; if you can picture moments of joy and exhilaration when you truly have control over a wild and beautiful creature then start at the North American Falconers Association, or check here to find everything you can to educate yourself about the sport before you begin:

https://www.americanfalconry.com/link.html

Fishing

Fishing, also called angling, originated as a means of providing food, along with hunting, when men were really men and women were just as tough.

Anyway, fishing, which includes spear fishing, fly fishing (and fly tying), bone fishing, and ice fishing, is one of the world's most popular hobbies. It's relaxing and can actually contribute to local environmental conservation. Many fishermen are passionate about keeping water clean.

Some fishermen say that the most important reason to fish is that it's a natural stress buster. Spending time outdoors is freeing. Whether casting for trout or bobber fishing at a pond, fishermen aren't engaging with technology and work demands. It's an opportunity for many to bond with friends.

Fishing can also be a thrilling activity; some fish fight hard. Reeling in a marlin can take hours, and imagine the effort to land a 300-pound grouper. Imagine, too, the satisfaction.

There are so many varieties of fishing, it's important to consider your wants and needs first. Do you live in a northern climate where ice fishing is possible during winter? Do you like the idea of learning how to fish with a spear? Spear fishing can be accomplished almost anywhere, and some participants take it up a notch by spear fishing from a paddle board. Fly fishing can be enjoyed anywhere—from a boat, lake shore, or in ocean waves. Tying flies is an additional pastime that many fly fishermen enjoy.

To learn more about fishing, visit www.TakeMeFishing.org or www.aa-fishing.com to find a fishing club or organization near you.

Flying

Is flying dangerous? Of course, it can be. There are many risks associated with flying a plane. That said, enjoying life to its fullest implies a willingness to assume some reasonable risks associated with this hobby.

Flying safely requires learning how to fly from a reputable and licensed instructor and putting in the required hours to become licensed. Statistics say the average risk is about 6.6 accidents (and a fatality) for every 100,000 flight hours. Learn and use prudent practices when flying a plane. Don't skimp on the steps you will learn in flight training.

Getting a pilot's license is expensive. According to AOPA, the average individual spends about $10,000 on equipment rentals, instructor fees, and incidental costs associated with the process. The time required to get a pilot's license depends on the type of pilot you want to be. Choose from private, recreational, or sport pilot license.

D.L. Haley

You'll need about 40 hours for a private license, 30 hours for a recreational license, and 20 hours for a sport license.

For more information about flying a private plane, glider, or helicopter, visit the Aircraft Owners and Pilots Association at http://aopa.org/.

Gardening

Perhaps this doesn't strike you as a manly undertaking at first, but think about it. For thousands of years men have turned over the earth and planted seeds in order to provide sustenance for their clan. In latter centuries, they've also gardened for aesthetic pleasure.

My dad, a great man among men, was an avid gardener. He used to give talks on "postage stamp" gardening – the ability to grow a lot of vegetables in a very small space. Point being, you don't have to have a lot of land to grow things. In fact, you can build garden boxes or use pots for growing.

Dad also had a flair for roses and – I'm almost embarrassed to tell you this – gnomes. People used to come from all over to see his rose garden and all the gnomes in their pointy hats, fishing in the goldfish pond or just hanging out and, in a couple of cases, giving rude gestures.

Many of the world's most brilliant men combined intellectual pursuits with gardening. Thomas Jefferson, the third U.S. president, was known for his incredible gardens. The gardens at Monticello are still amazing because master gardeners work hard to keep everything just the way Mr. Jefferson designed it.

There are very practical reasons to enjoy gardening. Here are some of the most important reasons you should garden:

- The food from your garden is clean: That's right. You know what's in this food. If you plant organic seeds in organic soil, there's no question. It's organic.
- Growing food saves money. Have you priced organic produce today?
- Your garden will impress the one you love. Imagine cooking a meal for two from your garden! Add candlelight…
- Gardening inspires self-sufficiency. Once you start gardening and growing your food, you'll find other ways to do more with less. Really.
- Gardening will give you a hot body. It's great exercise. The act of planting, weeding, harvesting, and pulling/lifting will give you a workout.
- Gardening is meditation. Your mind will calm as you garden. You might even feel gratitude for the natural world. Reconnecting to nature is priceless.

To get started with gardening, visit your community garden or land trust. The American Horticultural Society (www.ahs.org/gardening-resources/societies-clubs-organizations/organizations) has an extensive list of garden associations to interest you.

D.L. Haley

Gold panning

"I know what gold does to men's souls." - Howard (the old prospector) in The Treasure of the Sierra Madre.

Do thoughts of shiny nuggets cause you to break out in a cold sweat? Do you envision yourself finding gobs of gold in a fast moving stream? Then you probably have gold fever. The condition can strike at any time. There's no cure, but it can be controlled by swirling dirty water in a pan and looking for flecks of yellow.

Modern day prospectors can practice their skills from Colorado to Georgia and Alaska. Gold panning and digging for gems are great ways to add the element of treasure hunting to your outings. If you're fishing for salmon in the Pacific Northwest, why not pan for gold as well?

North Georgia's Loud Mine, a commercial gold mine, is a place to improve your chances of panning for gold. You're unlikely to find gold nuggets here but tiny grains of gold are possible! Visit www.goldngemgrubbinstore.com to learn about Georgia's Dahlonega gold belt and how to pan for gold. Or check out the possibilities in North Carolina: www.goldmaps.com/east/north_carolina_gold.htm. It's also possible to find rubies, sapphires, and garnets here.

Here's a list that will help you locate gold mines around the USA:

http://www.detectorprospector.com/gold-prospecting-public-sites/sites/public-mining-site-list.htm

Hobbies for Men

Before you pan for gold or dig for gems, you may be able to find gold maps or gem maps of the area you're visiting. Visit www.geology.com for gold or gem maps.

Hot air ballooning

There are two ways to go with this: visit sites where you can pay to be taken up, or buy a balloon of your own.

Even if you've got dreams of ballooning around the world, this isn't a daily hobby. Most people never get the chance to experience ballooning so, if you're ready to step up to the task, it's an ideal way to combine relaxation or adventure. If you're the pilot, you probably won't find ballooning as relaxing as a passenger!

Balloons have three basic components:

- The envelope holds air needed for buoyancy.
- The basket holds standing pilot and passenger(s).
- The burner is the engine and moves heated air to the envelope.

Costs of ballooning aren't inexpensive. Plan to pay up to $300 per person to be taken on a balloon ride. Buying your own airship will set you back thousands. A new sport-sized rig will go for about $20,000; commercial balloons cost up to $60,000. Used balloons can be a lot less. A 1979 Aerostar Rally II was recently for sale at $4,000. Be careful with older models, though. I knew a guy whose balloon collapsed the second time he flew it. Fortunately, he hadn't risen very high and only suffered a broken leg. The balloon was laid to rest.

Hot air ballooning is regulated by the FAA; pilots must be licensed and balloons must pass regular inspections. Pilots are also required to have ground crews and insurance. The good news is you'll be in elite company. There are only a few thousand balloonists in the USA.

To find out more about ballooning, balloon rides, and programs to learn ballooning, visit the Balloon Federation of America at www.bfa.net or visit www.usairnet.com/hot-air-balloon/organizations/ to find a ballooning organization in your state.

Kayaking

Not the same as rowing. Kayakers sit facing the way they are going and use only one paddle. Kayaks also have a covered bow and stern, or for use in rapids will be completely covered so you zip yourself in. The sport offers unique opportunities to develop physical endurance and mental calm. Paddling a lake or slow-moving river can promote a sense of calm and peace, or go for the intensity of whitewater kayaking.

According to the History Channel, humans have been kayaking for thousands of years. Today, the numbers of extreme sports enthusiasts and nature lovers in kayaks have prompted retailers like L.L. Bean to offer kayaking courses in some locations. Some state parks also offer kayak rentals. According to a spokeperson at Nockamixon State Park (Bucks County, PA), "kayak rentals have increased hundreds of percent in the past few years."

Not only super-fit men enjoy kayaking. Because kayaking is a low impact sport, it's possible for average people with paddling skills to enjoy the sport:

- Paddling a kayak builds upper body strength and works the shoulders, back, arms, and chest.
- Depending upon the kayaker's speed, kayaking at slow speeds can also reduce stress.
- Kayaks are easy to transport and can be carried by one person. A canoe, in comparison, may require two people to move it. There's no need to haul a

kayak: it's relatively easy to put in the back of a pickup truck or strap to a roof rack.

- Fishermen enjoy combining kayaking and fishing, and some kayaks are specifically designed for this purpose. There's no need to worry about finding a boat ramp or water depth, either.
- Kayaking is a water sport. A personal flotation device (PFD) is an essential safety requirement for each person in the kayak. Young people may be required by state law to wear a life jacket.

Some state or local regulations require kayakers to purchase permits and display decals so, before kayaking, check requirements in your area. To learn more about kayaking, visit www.Paddling.net for a list of kayaking clubs and associations.

Marathon running

Long distance running can be a lifelong hobby. Most runners must train carefully—and over a considerable period of time—to run 26.2 miles.

If you're already a runner, don't rush to add mileage to your daily run. For instance, if you run three miles a day and want to become a marathon runner, give your body time to adjust to longer distances. Both mental and physical endurance are needed to complete a marathon.

Runner's World recommends slowly adding to a minimum running base of three to six months (running at least four times a week). It's better to build a running base over a longer period of at least a year to reduce the chance of injuries as mileage is increased. You should have a running base of about 15 – 20 miles per week and build to 35 – 40 miles before a marathon.

- If you've already been a runner for years and want to add marathon running to your repertoire, start with a base of about 35 miles and then peak before the marathon date at about 50+ miles.
- Don't increase your weekly miles by more than 10 percent in any week of training. Even if you feel great, adding miles too soon can encourage injury. For instance, if you run 20 miles a week now, don't run more than 22 miles in the first marathon training week.
- Part of your marathon training plan should include a single easy-pace "long run" (in relation to the total miles that week). Over your training schedule, plan to build the long run to 18 – 20 miles to prepare you for the marathon.

Provided you avoid injury, marathon running need not be expensive. The entry fee for most races is reasonable, though to register for the New York marathon you'll have to pay upwards of $250 (that's if you even get accepted). Shoes can cost from $50 to $200 or more. To learn more about marathon running or becoming a runner, visit www.runnersworld.com or the Road Runners Club of America at www.rrca.org/.

D.L. Haley

Motorcycling/BMX biking

Exploring the open road with a band of leather-clad brothers and 150 plus of horsepower between your legs - gets your testosterone going just thinking about it. But, you'll need a sharp mind, quick reflexes and a willingness to live a little dangerously.

All bikes are not created equal. Cruisers – like Harley Davidson – have a laid-back riding position, usually a big engine and are made for, well, cruising the highway. Sportbikes are high performance, high speed machines requiring skillful handling. Dubbed "crotch rockets" by some, presumably because of the intense feeling of power riders may experience.

Dual-sports are basically dirtbikes that are street legal. They are a good starter bike because of their light weight and smaller engines. Touring bikes are designed for long-distance travel, and then there's the Standard, which is probably the best beginner bike. It's an all-around kind of bike, usually with an upright riding position.

Keep in mind that before you hit the road you will need to be licensed. Each state has their own motorcycle riding requirements, so check with your local DMV.

According to the American Motorcyclist Association, a stunning 95 percent of motorcyclists are male. Purchase of motorcycles is on the rise. For instance, U.S. motorcyclists bought almost 500,000 motorcycles in 2014, up about 4 percent from 2013 sales.

Most owners use their motorcycle about 100 days a year but a hardy 13 percent ride their motorcycles more than 300 days of the year. Some go long distances by motorcycle, with 29 percent riding at least 10,000 miles a year. Almost half of long distance riders prefer a touring bike for that reason. Some use a motorcycle to commute to work. About 75 percent of motorcyclists take a course to learn how to drive a motorcycle.

To learn more about motorcycling, visit the American Motorcyclist Associate website at www.americanmotorcyclist.com.

BMX gaming, on the other hand, is enjoyed by racers. The first BMX race happened in 1974 (the Yamaha Gold Cup). The very first BMX bike was created by Schwinn in 1963. Soon, tricks like the 360 midair spin or "going freestyle" was happening around the country. The documentary, "Joe Kid on a Sting-Ray" is a great place to start if learning about BMX appeals to you.

If you're interested in BMX biking, find the right bike first. The American Bicycle Association (ABA) or National Bicycle League (NBL) sites are a good place to begin researching the best bikes.

Paddle Boarding

Continues to rise in popularity. According to Outdoor Foundation, paddle boarding participants have increased more than 300 percent between the years of 2010 to 2014. About 3 million paddle boarders participated in the sport (2014), in comparison to about one million paddle boarders in 2010. About 55 percent of standup paddle boarding (SUP) is enjoyed by men, which means a lot of women are out there too.

Now think about this, guys. You have an opportunity to flex your manly muscle in front of your favorite lady while paddling and talking about your dreams to save abandoned puppies and create technology to remove trash from the World's oceans. This is one reason it's cool to paddle board these days.

Paddle boarding is considered easier to learn than similar sports such as windsurfing or snowboarding. There's no need to go to a particular geographic location or climate to practice it. Paddle boarding can be performed in almost any body of water, including oceans, rivers, and lakes. Almost 75 percent of paddle boarders are aged 40 or less.

Historians say that today's paddle boarding can be traced to Hawaiian surfers. Paddles were used by surfers to exercise in calm ocean waters without waves. It's been popular in the Pacific islands for at least 10 years.

Paddle boarding requires an investment in a board and paddle:

- High performing, slim paddle boards can cost $2,000 or more, but it's possible to get an inexpensive paddle board for less than $500.
- An average paddle board costs about $1,000.

- Many paddle boarding enthusiasts have more than one board. Some retailers also carry convenient inflatable paddleboards for the occasional paddle boarder.
- Some paddle boarding participants enjoy fishing from a paddleboard (e.g. SUP fishing) or practicing yoga positions on a sturdy board.

Perhaps the best reason to paddleboard is that it can be an ultra-competitive sport—or not. Although many runners and triathletes like paddle boarding (and compete in paddle boarding races), it's possible to enjoy low-key paddle boarding at one's own pace. To learn more about how to get started in paddle boarding, contact a local paddle board fitness program or the World Paddle Association at www.worldpaddleassociation.com.

Rock climbing

If you're looking for a real adrenaline rush, this could be for you. Rock climbing is frequently considered an extreme hobby as opposed to mountaineering, which begins with casual treks through the mountains.

There are several different types of rock climbing:
- It's possible to begin rock climbing indoors on a climbing wall. If interested in rock climbing, the novice learns "moves" to effect solutions needed to climb a rock face.
- Bouldering is needed to progress in rock climbing. The rock climber uses moves he or she has

learned to move up the short-face of a boulder, rock or ice wall.

• More rock climbers prefer to climb without a harness. Instead, a mat or "crash pad" is in place to break a fall if it happens. (This preference has grown in popularity over the past 20 to 30 years.)

According to the Outdoor Recreation Participation Report performed by the Outdoor Foundation (2010), rock climbing, bouldering, sport climbing, and mountaineering participants are increasing in the U.S. About 9 million participants were identified as rock climbers and mountaineering enthusiasts in the study, up about two percent from previous data collected by the Coleman Company:

• About 5 million participants focus on natural rock climbs

• Almost 7 million enjoy artificial wall climbing: younger males prefer this sport

• Approximately one million participants focus on ice climbs

On average, rock climbing or mountaineering enthusiasts are male (outnumbering women two to one), young (less than 30) and live in the Western United States. Interestingly, many rock climbers also like bicycling, fishing, trail-running, and hiking. About a third of rock climbers save for just one event a year.

Almost 30 percent of participants report household income of more than $80,000, with most participants reporting between $40-79,000 per year. Visit the Outdoor

Foundation website at www.outdoorfoundation.org to learn more about rock climbing and mountaineering.

Sailing

The first person (that we know of) to sail solo around the world was Joshua Slocomb in his boat Spray, in 1898. These days there's a bunch of people who have accomplished the same feat, including teenagers. You may not aspire to be one of them or wish to face four-story-high waves and mechanical breakdowns in a vast, lonely ocean, but you can still enjoy the thrilling sensation of rushing wind and speeding across bright water.

It's possible to rent a sailboat in many parts of the country. Before you dive in and buy your own sailboat (and deal with where to keep your boat or store it in the winter, along with a lot of expense), consider renting a sailboat or using a friend's boat first.

Sailing is a hobby that will boost your physical fitness (your abs, legs, and arms will get very strong the more you sail) and can also relax you. Sail alone if you need me-time, or bring family and friends.

There's an important mental performance element to sailing, too. Because you must constantly assess the environment around you, including other boats and the elements, sailing can be a challenging hobby. For instance, is that just a bit of wind or a breeze before the storm?

If sailing is something you want to enjoy, learn more at:

D.L. Haley

- The United States Sailing Association at www.ussailing.org
- The American Sailing Association (ASA) at https://asa.com
- Your local sailing association

Scuba diving

Scuba may be an ideal geek hobby; a way to get in touch with your macho self. There are plenty of cool tech gadgets, toys, and data processors to use when you're under the sea. Because there's an exclusive potential to see, find, and do something very few other people do, scuba diving is an elite hobby that many in the technical field seem to value. Because you're required to leave the house or office to go scuba diving, and because the aquatic medium separates you from work and life technology, it's a perfect way to unplug.

When diving, the decision of what to think about and explore is up to you. Take photographs, watch wild life, look for sunken treasure or artifacts, or consider physics. To obtain scuba certification—necessary to get equipment needed to scuba dive, visit the certifying agency sites:

- Professional Association of Diving Instructors (PADI) at https://www.padi.com
- National Association of Underwater Instructors (NAUI) at https://www.naui.org

Snowboarding

A complete lack of fear combined with natural athletic ability are not absolutely necessary for snowboarding, but they sure as heck will help. Oh, and youth helps too.

Most snowboarders are between the ages of 25 to 34. Slightly less than 12 percent are older than age 34. Most snowboarding participants are also well-educated, with SIA (Snowsports Industries America) saying that at least half of participants hold a bachelor or graduate degree.

Snowboarding is most popular in the Rockies and Northeast. Average Rocky Mountain area snowboarders enjoy more than 20 snowboarding visits a year.

Northeastern participants enjoy about 13 snowboarding visits each year. Maine has the highest snowboarding participation per capita. Snowboarding seems to have declined in the U.S. Pacific region, falling from a high of about 12 visits in 2001 to around 7 visits in 2015.

Snowboarding is an expensive sport. Participants must purchase equipment, outerwear, apparel/accessories, and equipment/accessories:
- An average snowboard costs about $300.
- Snowboard boots cost an average of $160.
- Snowboard bindings cost an average $148.

According to Statistics Brain, snowboarding peaked in the U.S. in 2007 with 6.1 million participants with an average income of $100,000 or more. The site reports about 5.675 million participants now. About 20 percent of snowboarding enthusiasts also ski.

Snowboarding is a potentially dangerous sport. Fatalities and serious injuries (such as paralysis or head injuries) are reported each season. It's important to check equipment and keep it in good repair. Take a look at http://www.snowboarder.com/ for more.

Spelunking

Also called caving, spelunking involves exploring caves and cave systems. People who actually study caves and cave environments practice the science of speleology.

Some people consider spelunking a type of extreme sport. In part, the extreme quality of spelunking depends on the caves you plan to explore. If you're exploring a cave that has little light once you're past the entrance, water hazards, and narrow squeezes, that's extreme adventure tourism at the very least. Before you go spelunking, do your homework and avoid dangerous caves, or be sure to go with experienced cavers.

To learn more about spelunking and speleology, visit the National Speleological Society (USA) at www.caves.org.

Storm chasing

Recreational storm chasers pursue severe weather for the challenge and adventure of traveling hundreds of miles to witness and document nature's fury. If you're lucky, you might even be able to sell some of your photographs or video to other enthusiasts or get your footage on the news.

This is a hobby that requires only a reliable vehicle (some chasers do customize their vehicles), camera, common sense and some guts. Although you're going to approach storm chasing in a responsible manner and not take chances, the weather can be very dangerous and unpredictable. Even a small storm can drop a lightning bolt without warning, so this is not for the faint of heart.

A good resource for storm chasers is http://www.stormchaser.com where you can even find links on taking a storm chase tour.

D.L. Haley

Surfing

No longer a fringe hobby sport these days, Surfrider Foundation reports there are about 3.3 million U.S. surfers (2015) who enjoy surfing about 108 times per year (spending about $40 per surfing experience). The average surfer has been surfing for 16 years and is now 34 years old.

Almost 90 percent of surfers are male. (Machismo dominates!). Surfing requires strength, balance and flexibility, attributes that many women possess, but apparently machismo dominates in the sport. On the other hand, women seem to be particularly attracted to hot surfer dudes, and that's certainly an incentive for guys to get into this hobby.

An average surfboard costs about $750. It is possible to rent a surfboard in some areas. An average longboard can cost up to $1,300. Shortboards cost less, around $600. It's possible to buy a used surfboard, and getting a fair price on a used board leaves more money for wetsuits and other items needed to enjoy a surfing hobby.

Some surfing enthusiasts make their own surfboard. According to Stab Magazine, the average surfboard costs about $250 to create from fiberglass and polyester materials.

The average surfer owns four surf boards and has a college bachelor or graduate education. Most surfers travel a median distance of 10 miles to surf and enjoy 2.5 hours per surf session.

For those of you who are politically active and seek to protect waves and coastal resources, surfing may have added appeal. For example, Surfers Against Sewage (UK) wants to raise awareness about the economic importance of clean water.

For more information about surfing, visit Surfer Magazine at www.surfermag.com and Surfrider Foundation at https://www.surfrider.org.

Survivalism

Talk about a hobby that can save your life. Since it's necessary to develop many skills in order to call yourself a full-fledged survivalist, don't allow yourself to get overwhelmed. Instead of learning backpacking and camping, firearms shooting, martial arts (self-defense), cooking, off-road driving, archery, hunting/fishing, and auto mechanics all at once, create a plan to expand skills you have, like some cooking, with camping.

When you're cooking, you want to assemble a meal with whatever's on hand. Don't waste food — make a meal of leftovers. Use charcoal grilling from time to time, too. In an emergency, you might not have electric or gas to cook with. And on the trail you will need to know how to find clean water and how to find safety.

You get the idea. Survivalism isn't about paranoia. Instead, survivalists prepare for the worst while enjoying the benefits of living in today's world. Learning to reuse, repurpose, and repair what you have is more than a handy skill, too. You'll save money.

To learn more about survivalism, check out the American Preppers Network at http://americanpreppersnetwork.com/.

Target Shooting

From the days of Buffalo Bill to youtube sensations of today (yep, there's a guy who can shoot an aspirin off a balloon backwards), target-shooting, including handgun, rifle, shot gun, Skeet shooting, and more, has been a fulfilling hobby for millions of men. According to research collected by the National Shooting Sports Foundation (NSSF), more than 20 million people in America enjoy shooting sports. More than 60 percent of target-shooting enthusiasts are male. The average target shooter is 33 years old, lives in an urban or suburban area, and began shooting in some form after he or she turned 18.

Target-shooting and shooting sports activities are typically performed using handguns (plinking/informal; sighting-in; training-related; testing; bullseye; silhouette high power; silhouette rimfire; cowboy action; IPSC; and other), rifles (plinking/informal; sighting-in; benchrest; long-range; training; tactical; silhouette rim fire; silhouette high power; cowboy action; three position; NRA high power; silhouette black powder; other) and shotguns (sighting-in; sporting clays; trap; skeet; informal shooting; cowboy; five-stand; test-related; other).

The average annual cost of participating in target-shooting was about $493 a year in 2011. Target-shooters in California, Texas, Pennsylvania, New York, and Florida spend the most on the sport. Visit the National Shooting Sports Foundation Inc. website at www.nssf.org/shooting/sports/orgs.cfm to learn more.

White water rafting

Punters (not football, but people who propel a flat-bottomed boat with a pole), it's time to meet your big, bad cousin, white water rafting.

Sure, there are several grades of white water rafting, called Classes, and Class 1 is for beginners or inveterate sissies, with very small areas of rough water requiring little maneuvering and no skill. The real manly man will work his way up to a class 5 or even 6, which is considered so dangerous it's almost unnavigable. Rafters will brave huge waves, shocking drops, rocks and hazards to test the limitations of both man and equipment. Chances of injury or even death are pretty high, so don't even consider white water rafting unless you're in tip top condition and have a fair dose of courage.

The cost of white water rafting depends upon the location. The Outdoor Foundation says that the average per person single trip cost is about $50 on weekdays and about $90 dollars on weekends. Google reports that an average trip is $25 to $115, dependent upon the location and season of the trip. Some white water rafting trips also include extras, such as bank-side barbecues. Costs to participate in a multi-day white water rafting trip are higher.

Since many participants also engage the services of a guide, the cost of frequent white water rafting may be prohibitive. Most white water rafting participants (34 percent) report household incomes of $100,000 or more. Half earn between $75-100,000+. About 60 percent of white water rafting enthusiasts are male. About 42 percent of all participants are college graduates: 16 percent hold graduate degrees.

Because white water rafting isn't a sustainable fitness activity, most participants report walking, hiking, fishing, bicycling, or sports to achieve fitness. Many report the use of fitness equipment, including weights (40 percent), treadmill (31 percent), resistance machines (29 percent) or elliptical machines (21 percent) in addition to other aerobic activities.

One of the best experiences for white water rafting is the Colorado River in Arizona, where you'll see the Grand Canyon like never before. Be advised, however, you may have to book up to two years in advance. The Gauley River in West Virginia offers 35-miles of Class 5 and above rapids combined with a remote landscape. Alaska's glacial Nenana River will give you a chilly thrill from Mt. McKinley northwards, and a chance to catch sight of some amazing wildlife.

Unusual

Bad movies

I can't deny, this is one of my favorite pastimes. Anyone see Battlefield Earth with John Travolta as a ten-foot alien sporting dreadlocks? Or how about The Giant Claw? This one's hysterical with the evil creature looking like an oversized Muppet.

You can watch bad movies and laugh out loud. If some of your favorite movies are bad movies, that's okay. RottenTomatoes.com was originally conceived as a review site for bad movies. A zero percent rating on Rotten Tomatoes is obviously a really bad movie.

If you like bad movies, it's easy to get suggestions from friends and acquaintances. For instance, if you're a father of small children, your friends probably tell you what not to watch with your kids. A low budget film called The Princess and the Pea sounded like a good bet. Nah!

You can easily spot some bad movies by their titles: The Wrestling Women vs. the Aztec Mummy, Frankenhoover, Leprechaun in Space, and Bloodsucking Freaks are all really bad, which makes them pretty great for bad movie aficionados.

D.L. Haley

Bricklaying

Among his many interests and pastimes, Sir Winston Churchill was a skilled bricklayer. There's a story to this. Churchill suffered a devastating political defeat; the sort of thing that many do not recover from. But, being a manly man, Churchill didn't just mope, he learnt to be a bricklayer, even getting his certification. Oh, and later he went back to politics, became Prime Minister of Great Britain and saved Europe from the Nazis.

Now, I can't say for sure that bricklaying would have that kind of therapeutic effect on you, but it did for someone else I know – my dad. He would tell you that it is incredibly satisfying to build something solid and enduring that is also useful and artful.

Bricklaying isn't just about walls. Build an outdoor grill, brick oven, mailbox, something for the kids. You'll find plenty of information online about bricklaying, though much of it is from the UK. And as an extra, you might get into the hobby of brick collecting. Seriously, there are antique bricks you can find to incorporate into your structures.

Extreme ironing

This has to be one of the all-time silliest hobbies ever, which means you'd have to be manly in order to participate because you'll certainly be the butt of a lot of jokes. That said, extreme ironers perform some incredible, and dangerous, feats in pursuit of their craft, from sky dive ironing to mountain top ironing. The official website – which no longer exists (makes you wonder) - described extreme ironing as the "latest danger sport that combines the thrills of an extreme outdoor activity with the satisfaction of a well pressed shirt."

OK, enough said. Take a look at some extreme ironing examples here:

http://www.gadling.com/2010/03/22/ten-best-extreme-ironing-stunts-from-around-the-world/.

D.L. Haley

Geocashing

Geocashing is a kind of real life treasure hunt that uses GPS devices. You use GPS coordinates to find a geocache container that's hidden. To get started with geocaching, you register at the https://www.geocaching.com website. A basic membership is free.

Once you're logged into the site, search for geocaches according to your post code. Then you select a geocache from the site list and click on it. The GPS coordinates are displayed—just enter them into your device.

If all goes well, you find the container with your GPS. You should sign your name in the geocache log and put the geocache back the way you found it. It's usually ok to leave something in the geocache of equal/greater value if you take something with you.

Take photos of the geocache and share them. If you're so inclined, tell others about the adventure in the post. It's part of the fun.

Ghost hunting

If sitting in the dark talking to dead people strikes you as appealing, then you should consider ghost hunting as a hobby. Don't just learn about the unexplained mysteries of the world; become a part of them.

Experienced ghost hunters recommend you join an established organization on a hunt before you go it alone. Apart from the benefit of their expertise, there are some mean spirits out there and an amateur could come to harm.

The Society for Paranormal Investigation says that ghost hunting is an expensive hobby because of the equipment and training necessary to hunt ghosts. It's difficult to make money at ghost hunting, and successful ghost hunting can take up lots of your time.

It's important to ask for spiritual protection before attempting to hunt ghosts. In addition to your physical equipment, don't forget to protect yourself from negative energies that some ghosts possess.

- Bring plenty of flashlights to an investigation. Each ghost hunter should have at least two flashlights or light sources at any time. Power drains can and do happen. A photon LED light worn around the neck can ensure that the ghost hunter always has light. For obvious reasons, don't use flammable light sources such as matches or candles.
- Along the same lines, bring rechargeable batteries for your flashlights or devices. A car charger, away from the ghost hunting site, can help you restore battery life if necessary. For instance, if you're hoping to record electronic voice phenomena (EVP), you'll need lots of battery life to keep digital records going for hours or days if necessary.

- Bring pen and paper to a ghost hunt because you can't assume that electronic devices will work. Small notepads and writing implements are best. Bring extras.

Lock picking

Admittedly, it's unlikely you've considered this as a hobby, but you never know when it might be useful. What if your wife accidentally locked the new puppy in the garden shed on a hot day, and you can't find the key that came with the door? You use your Sherlockian (Sher "lock" – get it?) skills to free the pooch and suddenly you're a hero. Nice going, big man.

On a serious note, learning lock picking can help you understand locks and security and how to protect (or fail at protecting) your possessions.

Locksport International (www.locksport.com) is a lockpicking organization. If you're interested in lockpicking or want to socialize/network with others interested in lockpicking, you'll find many useful resources there. www.Lockpicking101.com is another useful resource, and get a copy of Practical Lock Picking, by Deviant Ollam.

Jousting

Oh, yeah. The thunder of hooves, the clash of wood on steel. Why hang with the peasantry when you can ride high in chivalry?

Actually, the idea of chivalric knights jousting for the love of a fair maiden isn't really what it's all about. Back in the middle ages, when nobles provided knights to fight for their king, jousting was a way to sharpen combat skills, improve horsemanship and keep in fighting shape. By around 1066 (yep, the same year as the Battle of Hastings), jousting tournaments had become popular entertainment. Today's tournaments offer a glimpse into courtly life and the mores of Medieval times.

Jousting is definitely a manly sport - although a few women participate these days – and it's dangerous. Two riders charge at each other, colliding at 30 miles an hour. Bones get broken, to say nothing of damaged egos.

Competitive jousting could be for you if you have excellent riding skills, strength, focus, the ability to withstand pain and perhaps a bit of a death wish. Also, you will need to attain a certification before being able to participate in competition.

For those of you who are put off by the fact that jousting with actual heavy lances can be deadly, you may prefer to choose re-enactment or theatrical jousting. You can still be a knight in shining armor.

If you live in the Mid-Atlantic states of the USA, you may know that jousting is Maryland's official sport. Ring tournaments are held there each year. Calvert County's Jousting Tournament is widely anticipated each year. ESPN has featured the tournament in years past. Otherwise, most jousting participants enjoy re-enacting in Medieval or Renaissance fairs and tournaments that are held in the U.S. and around the world. Warwick Castle in the UK hosts jousting tournaments on an ongoing basis. The castle was originally the domain of William the Conqueror.

To learn more about jousting, including the necessary equipment, visit the International Jousting Association website at www.ija-usa.com, the National Jousting Association at www.nationaljousting.com, or The Jousting Life group on Facebook at https://www.facebook.com/TheJoustingLife.

Oh, and here's a little fact that might interest you. Sometimes nobles would hire a jouster who had no allegiance to any master. These part-time employees were known as "freelancers."

News-raiding

We've all seen the guy who seems to casually turn up in the background of news reports. Well, it may have been a carefully planned stunt.

News raiding evolved from photobombing. If you've ever popped into the background of someone else's picture and essentially ruined it, then you've photobombed. After photobombing came videobombing and now news-raiding, which involves inserting yourself into live newscasts. It's a good idea to wear something that easily identifies you every time you news-raid. You know, an ugly plaid shirt, a pork pie hat, seriously ugly eyeglasses, that sort of thing. One of the most well-known news-raiders is Paul Yarrow, a rather portly English chap who said he wanted to make a statement "about the image conscious media."

Robot making

Would you like someone to make your coffee, clean house, walk the dog or just be a companion? Create a robot. Are you interested in programming, electronics, controls, mechanics, behavior, and psychology? Make robots your hobby. With the use of online tutorials and texts, it's possible to teach yourself all about robot making. You'll start with something that probably isn't much more than a box on wheels, but the long-term possibilities are endless.

Like many hobbies, robot making can be expensive. According to the Society of Robots, plan to spend at least $100 to $200 for a first robot. If you're a college student, it's possible to look for a robotics internship. Working for a robotics company can defray costs of robot making.

Robotics clubs are another option. MIT's Robotics Team at the Edgerton Center in Cambridge, MA is an example. However, many high schools and 4-H clubs around the country have robot making groups.

Robot making is a fascinating hobby. To learn more about a robotics organization near you, visit www.roboticstoday.com.

Taphophilia

Taphophilia, or a passion for cemeteries, and gravestone rubbing are relatives of ghost hunting. The word originates from the Greek, "taphos," which means tomb, and another Greek word, "philos," meaning loving or dear. Taphophiles are sometimes labeled as "Tombstone tourists."

The hobby of taphophilia can involve gravestone rubbings, photographing graves and mausoleums, searching for the resting places of ancestors or famous people, or simply enjoying the tranquility of cemeteries.

There's not a lot of specific information online about taphophilia but this group may be of help to you: https://www.flickr.com/groups/taphophilia/. And here's a list of books you could check out: https://www.goodreads.com/list/show/14362.Must_Have_Cemetery_Books#453915.

Tomahawk and Axe throwing

So you picture yourself as a modern day mountain man. You're searching for a really manly or primal hobby. Well, this could be it.

Hobbies for Men

Contrary to what you might imagine, tomahawks and axes weren't thrown in battle. Think about it. You toss your 'hawk and maybe kill someone, but now you have no weapon. So mountain men and Indians used their hatchets for close combat and threw them mostly for fun.

Learning to throw a tomahawk or hatchet isn't easy, so you probably won't master the art of tomahawk (also known as 'hawk') throwing right away.

Enthusiasts say that getting a lightweight hawk or hatchet can make learning the hobby a bit easier. Some tips from those who've accomplished the art of throwing a hawk:

- Don't stand too far away from the piece of wood target you're aiming for. Stand about five paces away from the target.
- Begin by bringing the tomahawk in line with your ear. Your forearm should bend forward. Bend at the waist and follow the motion through by pointing the opposing hand at the target.
- Hold the tomahawk as you would a hammer before tossing it toward the target. Place your "throwing foot" forward while training an eye on the target, and swing the tomahawk up and down.
- Hurl the hawk in a straight motion towards the target.

Read through this manual on how to throw a tomahawk:

http://user.xmission.com/~drudy/amm/skills/hawkman.html.

D.L. Haley

Volcano boarding

Also called volcano surfing, is enjoyed by thrill seekers on volcano slopes. National Geographic reports that western Nicaragua's Cerro Negro slope (an active volcano) is one of the most popular for volcano boarders and surfers. It's considered an extreme sport because in the event of a volcanic eruption you risk death by lava. Ouch!

Mount Yasur (Vanuatu) is one of the most popular places for volcano boarding because the volcano has been active since the 18th century. Zoltan Istavan, an adventurer and writer, wrote about his experience there in 2002. National Geographic also filmed the experience. Istavan's first volcano boarding experience occurred in 1995.

You'll need some stamina for volcano boarding as it requires first hiking up the volcano and then sliding down, seated or standing, on a metal or plywood board.

If volcano boarding interests you, visit the Volcano Board site at www.volcanoboard.com or search for tour guides who specialize in volcano boarding and surfing experiences.

Whip cracking

With visions of Indiana Jones in my head I took a crack at using a whip and it's a lot harder than you might think. I managed the first couple of cracks but my manliness took a beating when I tried the figure eight and got the whip wrapped around my ankles.

With this hobby your primary cost is the whip. No doubt most of you are familiar with the bullwhip but, in actuality, there are lots of different types of whips of different lengths, materials, weights and plaits. Do your due diligence to find what best suits you and expect to pay upwards of $500.

Find a wide open and safe space (no people near) where you can hone your whip handling skills or look for a whip studio in your area (and I'm not referring to anything kinky). There aren't many around but if you're really serious about this hobby why not consider a vacation that revolves around training. You might even become good enough for sport whip cracking, which is gaining popularity. This might involve cracking sequences, cracking with two or more whips, hitting or cutting targets, moving and controlling targets.

Before you commit to this hobby, I suggest you read Let's Get Cracking!: The How-To Book Of Bullwhip Skills, by Robert Dante. It will give you a good overview of whip cracking and safety with illustrations.

Everything Else

Black powder cannons

Do you enjoy noise, power, history? Then this could be your ideal hobby. My interest in cannons was sparked (get it?) when I worked for a while with a shipwreck treasure hunter who had a number of antique cannon, from signal guns to hand-held and ship-board guns.

Black powder guns can run you the gamut of prices from about $50 for a newly-fabricated golf-ball mortar to tens of thousands for a restored antique. You can buy everything from backyard fabricated to signal guns to civil war replicas but for my money, half the fun is in finding old originals or used replicas in flea markets, antique stores, even ebay, though ebay is well-watched these days by collectors.

D.L. Haley

Not all guns are fireable. Antiques may appear sturdy but many of them were not particularly safe when they were made. Many of the Civil War cannon, for instance, were prone to explode. Do not even think of firing a gun unless you are absolutely sure it is safe to do so.

The absolute first thing you should do is research. Use the search term "black powder cannons" on google and a load of stuff will come up. Go to ebay but don't buy anything, just follow the auctions to get a sense of what sells best and at what prices. For antiques go here, http://www.gunsinternational.com, search for "cannon" and take a gander at what comes up.

Stop in to your library to see if they have any books on black powder cannons. Unfortunately, there's very little out there. I had a fairly extensive collection of books that I sold, which was not the smartest move I've ever made. Most of the books are long out of print and considered collectibles in their own right. *Cannons* by Dean S. Thomas is a small booklet that will get you started. There are several black powder books out there but mostly geared toward muzzle-loading rifles. Civil War enthusiasts might look for a copy of *Field Artillery Weapons of the Civil War*, it's probably available in facsimile.

Here's a very important note. Although black powder guns are legal in most parts of the USA be sure to check local laws. You may need a permit or license and will likely have restrictions on when and where guns can be fired.

Another very important point is to be sure you are well-versed in how to fire a black powder cannon before you even think of lighting a match. Again, look online and look for books. Most gun store owners are also usually more than happy to guide you. Consider also joining a black powder gun club for advice and guidance.

Car racing

This is a quintessential manly sport. Imagine the thrill when you're behind the wheel of a car going at 200 miles an hour.

There are various types of car racing so, if this is a hobby for you, start by deciding if you want to race open wheel, drag racing, NASCAR racing, or something else.

Before you make an investment in a car racing hobby, read everything you can about it. Watch televised races and go to car races. This investment in time will help you understand all aspects of racing, not just how to drive a race car.

Car racing typically involves more than a race car driver. You need to access the skills of mechanics and perhaps crew members. One of the best ways to learn about car racing is to work with a crew or even work at a racetrack. Get hands-on experience with race cars in any way you can.

Another way to learn about car racing is to attend a car racing school. A racing school teaches the basics as well as race car mechanics. School clubs can be a great way to get started in car racing.

Acquiring advanced methods of maneuvering a race car can take a life time. For more information about how to get started in car racing, Road and Track recommends outreach to one or more car racing schools, including Bondurant School of High Performance Driving (Arizona), Skip Barber Racing School (New Jersey), Allen Berg Racing Schools (California), Team O'Neill Rally School (New Hampshire), and Bertil Roos Racing School (Florida).

Chess

When asked what makes a man sexy, women often reply that intelligence has great appeal. So if you feel you're lacking as a babe magnet, it's time to put your cerebral hat on and learn the game of chess.

Actually, chess has many benefits, women aside. By challenging the brain, it stimulates the growth of dendrites that allow faster neural communication. Both the left and right hemispheres of the brain become highly active during play, and one study has shown chess actually raises a person's IQ.

There's also evidence that brain games such as chess may help prevent Alzheimer's, foster growth in creative thinking and problem-solving, and improve memory and recall.

The World Chess Federation estimates that about 605 million people play chess around the world. Most of those players are well-educated college graduates with higher than average household incomes (about $121,000 as of the last report). Chess players are almost three times as likely to read The Wall Street Journal than people who don't play chess.

And going back to women – well, sort of - a recent article in Chess Magazine theorizes that more men than women excel at chess because the sexes are "hard-wired" differently. The debate is likely to continue but, for now, chess is a male-dominated tournament sport.

To learn more about the game of chess, visit The World Chess Federation at https://www.fide.com or Chess Network Company at www.chessnc.com.

Cigars

Cigars and smoking instruments like pipes and hookahs can be ideal for the man who wants or needs deep relaxation. Cigar clubs or lounges found in many cities are the perfect place to enjoy a cigar or fruity tobacco. There's no need to go outside to smoke!

Interestingly, people who neither smoke cigarettes nor have a daily smoking habit seem to enjoy the ritual of smoking cigars. There are techniques to enjoying a fine, slow-burning stogie, so do some reading-up and start at home. You don't want to be labeled an amateur the first time you mingle with aficionados.

Then there's the hookah – an oriental pipe that draws smoke through a long tube across water. Hookah bars are becoming more popular but be warned, some hookah bars can involve dancing. If you're a student, finding a hookah bar can help you avoid the issue of tobacco-free campus, too.

Cigars and smoking – pipes, hookahs, etc. – can also be a celebration of manliness. If the ideal appeals to you, learn more at:

- International Association of Cigar Clubs at http://www.cigarclubs.org/
- Cigar Association of America, Inc. at www.cigarassociation.org

To find hookah lounges or clubs, search online sites like Yelp.

Collectibles

Collecting is generally for the more cerebral guy. It can be quite generalized, for instance Civil War artifacts, or it might involve only a sub-genre such as Civil War tokens.

Almost anything can be collectible. You simply need the means, opportunity and interest to acquire your chosen objects. Because the list of collectibles is nearly endless, rather than go into detail about any specific items, here's a list of a few things that I think are particularly manly (and you won't find women's panties on it).

Militaria

Breweriana
Time pieces
Stamps
Coins
Sports memorabilia
Weapons
Antique tools
Arrowheads
Police and firefighter gear
Old maps
Shipwreck artifacts
Fountain pens

Combine demolition derby

First, you have to have a worn-out old combine, then you need to overhaul it so it's lighter and more maneuverable but with a reinforced header. Then you have to get into an arena with a bunch of crazy folk where you're all going to do your damndest to destroy each other's machines. And it's even better if you can give your combine a name, like "Crush You," or "Wreck On."

Getting into the spirit of a combine demolition derby usually involves decorating the combines. Often, the most amazing decoration gets a prize. Although not every combine demolition derby offers cash prizes, some enticing awards in the thousands of dollars are possible for winners. Most entrants, however, say they lose money in the effort; this is something they do for fun.

Injuries are rare in combine demolition derbies, but they do happen. If you're considering entering a derby, learn more about it at a state fair near you. Chuck Palahniuk's book, "Demolition: Stranger Than Fiction: True Stories," (2005) is another helpful resource.

Drones

In military parlance a drone is a UAV (Unmanned Aerial Vehicle), used primarily for surveillance and intelligence gathering where manned flight is considered unsafe. This is not the kind of drone we're discussing here.

Radio controlled (RC) drones come in many shapes and sizes and a huge range of prices. A simple toy drone could cost as little as $30, and isn't a bad way to test your flying skills before you invest a great deal more. A racing drone will likely set you back $400 to $500, and a camera drone could be $500 to $3000.

Typically, a drone will have four rotors – Quadcopters – and there are different completion levels of drones. An RTF (ready-to-fly) will come complete in the box; just take your Quad out, charge the battery and you're set to go. BNF (Bind-N-Fly) also come fully assembled but you'll need to get your own RC transmitter. An ARF (almost-ready-to-fly) UAV is more of a kit model that may not have all the components and will require some assembly.

For those of you who are really skilled, have a go at making your own drone. Enthusiasts have created everything from a drone that shoots fireworks to a "flying reaper" drone. Then there's Bart Jansen, who turned his dead cat Orville into a drone (I kid you not). Last I heard he's working on a cow!

Anyway, there's a lot to know about drones – including FAA regs - so if this is something that appeals to you, I recommend you search out a local club or racing meet and ingratiate yourself with some experienced operators. For online resources start here: http://www.modelaircraft.org/clubsearch.aspx . This site has lots of resources, including tutorials: http://www.dronethusiast.com/.

Home improvement

For many guys this is in your manly genes. Think of Bob Vila and "This Old House" to know that home improvement and renovation is your birthright.

There are many great resources to inspire your home improvement hobby. The DIY Network/HGTV and YouTube are great resources. Identify the home improvement project you want to accomplish and there are multiple how-to videos to help you prepare for and execute the task, and probably impress your mate.

Retailers can also offer support for your home improvement hobby. Lowe's Home Improvement, The Home Depot, and local stores are valuable resources. If you're in doubt about the right tools and materials, there's someone to ask. You're never alone.

D.L. Haley

To get started, visit:
- DIY Network at www.diynetwork.com
- HGTV Home Improvement Ideas & Tips at www.hgtv.com
- AOL Home Improvement at www.aol.com/finance/tag/home-improvement/

Model railroading

When I was a kid my friend and I used to spend time in the attic of his home, where his dad had built a model railway that covered the whole space. We weren't allowed to run the trains without the father to supervise. Still, we were fascinated with this miniaturized mobile world.

Thousands of model railroading enthusiasts meet each year at conventions where they share their passion for scale model railroading. Learn more about the national and regional conventions at the National Model Railroad Association website at www.nmra.org/conventions.

If you like the idea of building intricate networks and designing communities through which model railroads traverse, or you love the idea of building winter holiday miniature model railroads with family and friends, this is the hobby for you.

The NMRA site also provides an Introduction to Model Railroading at www.nmra.org/beginners-guide with step-by-step instructions for building your first model railroad. A shopping list of materials and tools you'll need is provided.

Hobbies for Men

If you're a visual learner, visit the Model Railroader Video Plus site at mrv.trains.com.

Pinball

Lights flash, speakers boom and numbers rise as the steel ball ricochets off bumpers and shoots down alleys while you try to control it with flippers. Nothing else matters, you're absorbed in the game of pinball. Popeye, Lord of the Rings, Indiana Jones, Goldeneye…pinball themes are limitless.

This is a hobby that seems to be really popular with techies because it's based on physics, and offers tactile and hands-on feedback. And it's competitive, which suits Type A personalities. The player must take time to interact with the machine and there are even competitive leagues you can join. It can take months to master some games but, with persistence, the player feels accomplished when he beats the pinball machine.

Pinball aficionados insist each machine has its own personality and plays differently for each person using it, and hardcore players may have hundreds of machines in their collections. To play pinball you can of course go to arcades and other public places, but to buy a machine you will most likely have to fork out a few thousand dollars, unless you get lucky on ebay. A refurbished Michael

D.L. Haley

Jordan pinball machine could set you back more than $50,000.

Learn more about competitive pinball at International Flipper Pinball Association (IFPA) at www.ifpapinball.com.

Restore a classic car

Even if you don't have the skills to do the restoration on an old car or you don't want to learn, you can find someone who will work with you. And driving around in a restored 1957 Porsche Speedster doesn't hurt the old machismo.

For those of you who are too financially challenged to deal with a Porsche take a look at http://www.hemmings.com. Right now there is a 1965

Hobbies for Men

Ford Thunderbird in need of some love, for $4,000, and a 1947 Pontiac Torpedo Sport Coupe that would definitely be a long-term project for $4,950. Keep in mind that the cheapest part of car restoration is buying the car. You will need money for parts, maybe a lot of money. Not only are some parts expensive but they can be very hard to find so you may have to advertise for them, possibly for a long time. In addition to the usual hammers and saws that you may have already, you will need an air compressor, welding machine, wire cutters and more.

And time is something else you will need in abundance along with patience and determination. I know more than a couple of people who have had cars under wraps for years waiting for them to begin a restoration project. So be sure this is what you want to do before you spend anything.

Don't forget you will have to have a secure inside space to work on your car. Your own garage is ideal, provided you have the space to spare. Think twice before renting anywhere; the monthly fees can really rack up.

A repair manual is a great bonus. They simply won't be available for every vehicle but start looking at Chilton DIY, http://www.chiltondiy.com/, and there's always ebay. I never cease to be amazed at some of the things that show up there. The good news is that if you buy right and do a fine restoration job there could be someone out there willing to pay you a profit for your efforts.

D.L. Haley

Plane spotting

Also called aircraft spotting, plane spotting is a hobby that combines photography and tracking movement of airplanes using airport information, air traffic control data, and airliner routes. Plane spotters use software and data applications, along with social media sites, to track aircraft.

Visit: FlightAware (www.flightaware.com), a software/data firm mobile app with free flight tracking capability of private/commercial airplanes in the U.S., Australia, New Zealand, and Canada; www.Seatguru.com for seatmaps of airlines (search by name and flight); and www.Airliners.net to access aircraft photos and an aviation forum.

Riding roller coasters

Roller coasters are a hobby for those who enjoy an adrenaline rush along with frequent ups and downs...and upside downs. If riding roller coasters is your hobby, you'll need to visit amusement parks and ride different roller coasters around the U.S. or around the world.

Theme parks and amusement organizations announce new roller coasters each year, but some people who enjoy riding roller coasters have their favorites. For instance, they know the Mindbender in Austell, GA or the Kentucky Rumbler in Bowling Green, KY. Other people

Hobbies for Men

want to ride the latest roller coasters and travel all over the world to experience the thrill of more twists, turns, and loops.

There's a hydraulic launch coaster in Abu Dhabi that reaches an incredible 149 miles per hour. It accelerates from 0 to 62 mph in two seconds, has a top height of 171 feet and generates 1.7 Gs. Personally, I prefer wooden roller coasters. Sure, they rattle you around a bit, but that just makes the experience more real.

To learn more about riding roller coasters, visit www.ultimaterollercoaster.com searchable roller coaster database.

Slot car racing

Do you like racing cars and model cars? Well, you'll like the competitive hobby of slot car racing. Slot (or miniature) cars, use 1:24 or 1:32 scale cars that are guided by grooves or slots in the track. Unlike many model cars, they are models of real autos. Some enthusiasts motorize model cars and others prefer to build slot cars from scratch.

Many slot car tracks are incredibly elaborate and look like miniature versions of competitive racetracks and courses. Many of these tracks include amazing details, including trees, buildings, and people.

For more information about slot racing, or if you're interested in competitive slot racing, visit the United Slot Racers Association (www.usraslots.com) or the

D.L. Haley

International Slot Racing Association (www.isra-slot.com) for more information.

Stand-up comedy

How often have you been told, "You could be a comedian?" So what if people were being sarcastic? Go on and prove you can do it, because it takes a man with major moxie to stand in front of a room full of strangers and make them laugh.

Many comedy clubs have open-mic events that encourage stand-up comedians to try out new material and interact with an audience, but get started with books, CDs, and DVDs of established comedians. Start with your favorites and watch them over and over until every nuance and gesture used by the comedian is discovered. Write down ideas for stand-up routines in the interim and try them out on friends and family. Practice and perfect until ready to perform on stage. Open-mic opportunities can make routines better, even when the audience is lukewarm or reacts negatively to it. That reminds me, you probably should bring a thick skin with you.

Most stand-up comedians keep a notebook and write down new funny ideas as they occur. The best comedic ideas are original, so don't try to copy someone else's style or routine. Fresh and original funny material is in high demand. Almost any topic can be funny, but it's important to keep topics appropriate to the audience.

Don't give up. If possible, attend writing seminars such as those at World Series of Comedy (Las Vegas).

For more information about stand-up comedy, visit www.theworldseriesofcomedy.com or local and college stand-up comedy websites, such as Iowa State University's Stand-Up Comedy Club. Look for local opportunities to practice stand-up comedy as often as possible.

Ventriloquism

Once mastered, ventriloquism is a hobby that fascinates others. Think about Edgar Bergen and "Charlie McCarthy" (or Mortimer Snerd and Effie Klinker). Shari Lewis mesmerized children in the 1960s with fluffy animals "Lamb Chop" and "Hush Puppy." In recent years, Taylor Mason with "Barack Obama" and "Paquito" have been appreciated by millions of viewers.

Sydney Vereker's classic "Ventriloquism as a Hobby and How to Make It Pay" (1938, republished 2006) is a good place to start. Vereker guides you through speaking (without moving your lips), throwing your voice, and acting exercises to sharpen your character(s).

Cybervent, an organization for ventriloquists at http://www.ventriloquist.org/ and The Art Career Project ("How to Become a Ventriloquist") are helpful resources.

Author's Notes

I'm a professional writer. I spend a lot of my time sitting at home in my pajamas writing about my thoughts and my feelings on everything from personal hygiene to the state of the economy. And I spend too much time staring at my computer monitor wondering what to write about next and feeling bored. That's why I need a hobby. Mine is writing books like this.

D. L. Haley

If you enjoyed Hobbies For Men, you might also like this book by D. L. Haley.

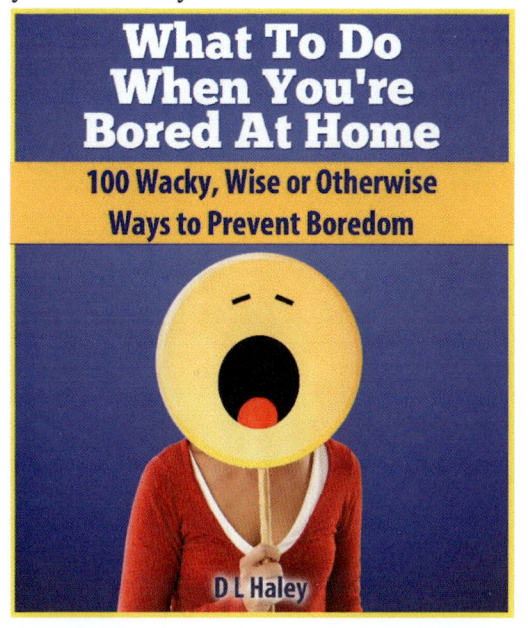

What To Do When You're Bored At Home
100 Wacky, Wise or Otherwise Ways to Prevent Boredom
D L Haley

Available at bookstores everywhere.

Printed in Great Britain
by Amazon